ISBN 978-1-331-43415-3
PIBN 10189692

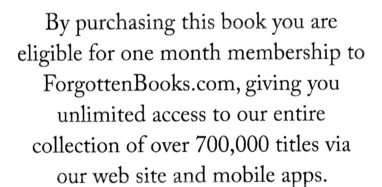

MEMOIRS

OF THE

DE-ISLAND BAR.

———

BY WILKINS UPDIKE, ESQ.

———

Knowles & Vose, Printers, Providence, R. I.

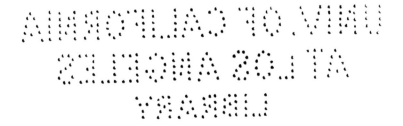

ERRATA.

Page 54, line 2 from top, for "1748" read 1741.

" 99, " 3 " bottom, for "Styles" read *Stiles.*

" 136, " 14 " " for "mata" read *mater.*

" 149, " 11 " " for "Lippett" read *Lippitt.*

" 165, " 8 " " insert *wrote* after Howell.

" 210, " 11 " top, for "collection" read *collocation.*

" 211, " 10 " bottom, for "domit" read *docuit.*

" 215, " 6 " top, for "without" read *with.*

" 217, " " " for "capitolenum" read *capitolium.*

" 220, " 2 " bottom, for "Centre" read *Senter.*

" 228, " 5 " top, for "Montesqueiu" read *Montesquieu.*

" 237, " 4 " bottom, for "amazing" read *amusing.*

" 243, " 6 " top, for "of" read *and.*

" 243, " 20 " " for "Mantimomah" read *Myantonomy.*

" 248, " 12 " " for "Styles" read *Stiles.*

The careful reader will detect several other errors, mostly in orthography and punctuation, but none, we believe, which will subvert or materially affect the meaning of the context. The publishers do not feel responsible for any imperfections in the work, as it did not come under their supervision whilst passing through the press.

CONTENTS.

1*

DEDICATION.

~~~~~~~~

TO ALBERT C. GREENE, ESQ.

ATTORNEY GENERAL OF RHODE-ISLAND.

DEAR SIR,—Most of the persons whose Memoirs are contained in the present volume, were your predecessors in office. That fact alone would indicate the propriety of its dedication to you.

But that is not my only reason for inscribing it with your name; I do it also as a testimony of warm personal regard; and am happy that this opportunity is afforded me of paying, at the same time, a tribute to official worth and private friendship.

W. UPDIKE.

PREFACE.

HAVING recently devoted some of my leisure hours to procuring materials for the Memoirs of the early members of the Rhode-Island Bar, and knowing that some of the profession have felt a deep solicitude in rescuing from oblivion the few incidents that remain of them, I have concluded to yield to their solicitations, and submit to the public those collected in this volume, as imperfect as I am apprehensive they must be. The occasional inquiry, of the younger members of the profession, respecting the characters and times of its early Advocates, has been an additional inducement for me to collect such facts and materials, as yet exist, of their history; hoping that the time is not far distant, when some mind more competent to the work, will improve upon the hints I have given, and do ample justice to their memories. The wholesome truth should be impressed upon all, that the citizen, and especially the public man, or the scholar, who is defectively informed upon the history or biography of his own country, is constantly liable to mortification and disability, however perfect may be his knowledge of other states and times.

In pursuing this biographical investigation, I have labored under serious and perplexing embarrassments, owing to the deficiency of the materials, to do justice to their characters. It must be observed, that in the life of a lawyer, there are scarcely any events that are

very impressive or imposing. If any were so, in the histories of
those portrayed, time has destroyed all evidences of them. Whatever was brilliant or splendid, passed off with the occasion that produced it. If they were eminent in their profession, others have
since existed, who to observers were probably as eminent if not more
so. Speeches, at that period, (with a single exception,) were not
reported; and nothing verbatim can now be procured. This redu-
ces their histories to short memoirs only. Still it seems incumbent
on us, as members of the same profession, to preserve the few incidents and reminiscences of them, that now exist, and to transmit to
the next generation, the characters they sustained, for integrity, virtue and talent. Natural geniuses existed then, as well as now; and
like brilliant meteors they dazzled, delighted and died. Probably
more native talent went into the profession, at that early period,
than now, in proportion to numbers; for native power and strength
of intellect were then more necessary to sustain the advocate. He
was not assisted by other sciences, as the profession is at this period;
nor could he be supported or helped along by reports and authorities, as lawyers are at the present time. It must be apparent, that
much which was then unknown to the student, can now be gleaned
from reported arguments, and from the opinions of learned Courts;
besides the vast number of elementary writings, and other productions, mooting and discussing all questions, and collating all authorities, which are poured upon the profession, through the cheapness
of the press. The labor of thinking, and of mental origination, is
greatly diminished by the rich productions emanating from learned
brethren, emulous of fame. Before the revolution, "Coke upon Littleton," "Doctor and Student," "Bacon and Sheppard's grand
abridgment," "Croke," "Vaug," "Salkeld," "Hardwick" and
"Strange's" reports, and "Cowell's" and "Jacobs'" law dictiona-
ries, were the principal authorities that were used. The lawyers'
library, like Petrarch's, could be transported in his saddle-bags. The

most eminent and successful in the profession, relied more upon intense mental application, than upon books and precedents. They habituated themselves to the most rigid study, and thought deep and long upon particular cases. Those who were gifted with strong native intellects, with nerve and constitution enough to bear up against such labor, succeeded; and those who were deficient in these sturdy attributes, flagged on the course. Like the competitors in the Olympic games, those who were victorious in the race, bore off the laurel; and the feeble or unfortunate fell in the trial, and were heard of no more.

The mode of arguing causes then, partook much more of the narrative character, than at the present day. The advocate before a jury, gave minutely the history of the case, and the character of the parties, and freely used familiar anecdote and popular illustration. Appeals to the passions of the triors, were the most powerful engines of success. When satire or anger was kindled against an adversary, it was a consuming fire. If a client had been unfortunate, or oppressed, the chord of sympathy was touched to tears. The principal business of the Court was to see *fair play* between the legal gladiators; and the judges, who sat to listen, rather than direct, esteemed themselves fortunate, if, by their silence, they escaped unwounded in the conflict. But it must be borne in mind, at the same time, that except in cases when circumstances called out such sturdy efforts, the manners of the bar, of that day, were highly dignified and courteous. In the progress of judicial history, and particularly, within a few years past, the pungent severity of the ancient practice has undergone a commendable relaxation. This ameliorating progress is onward; and the epoch is speedily approaching when the cause and its merits, and not the character of the parties, will be the only legitimate subjects of trial.

If the following short memoirs of some of the ancient members of the profession, possess sufficient worth to merit the approbation of those gentlemen who have encouraged the publication, and the members of the Bar generally, I shall esteem it an adequate recompense for all the time and labor that has been bestowed upon them.

THE AUTHOR.

KINGSTON, May, 1842.

INTRODUCTION.

UPON the first settlement of Rhode-Island, the inhabitants were governed by voluntary articles of association. Roger Williams obtained the first Charter for the Colony in 1643–4; but owing to the conflicting claims of jurisdiction, interposed by Massachusetts, Plymouth, and Connecticut, the people were obstructed in erecting a government under it, until 1647. In May, of that year, the inhabitants assembled at Portsmouth, and organized a government, under the provisions of the Charter, and elected a President of the Colony, and four assistants, one for each of the towns of Newport, Portsmouth, Providence and Warwick; and formed a body of laws.

In May, 1650, the Legislature, by the following act, first created the offices of Attorney and Solicitor General of the Colony, viz.:—

"It is ordered that this court appoint one Attorney General for the Colony, as also a Solicitor.—

2

That the Attorney General shall have full power
to implead any transgression of the State, in any
Court in the State, but especially, to bring all such
matters of penal Laws, to the trial of the General
Court of trials, as also for the trial of the officers
of the State, at the General Assemblies; and to
implead in full power and authority of the free
people of this State, their prerogatives and liberties:
and because envy, the cut-throat of all prosperity,
will not fail to gallop with its full career, let the
said Attorney be faithfully engaged and authorized
and encouraged; engaged for the people, by or in
the people's name, and with their full authority
assisted; authorized that upon information of trans-
gressions and transgressors of the laws, prerogatives
and liberties of the people, and their penal laws, he
shall under hand and seal, take forth summons from
the President or general assistant, to command any
delinquent, or vehemently suspected of delinquency,
in what kind soever, according to the premises, to
appear at the General Court, if it be thereunto
belonging, or to the General Assembly, in those
matters proper thereunto, and if any refuse to appear at that mandamus, in the State of England's
name, and the people of this State, he shall be

judged guilty, and so proceeded against by fine and penalty."

" It is ordered, that in case of prohibitions, (any concerning guns, powder, lead, &c. it being provided that such and such, or any one had a gun, &c.) or the Solicitor, *bona fide* in his own knowledge, do know or can swear, &c. that such a one, was possessed of a gun, &c. as his own proper goods, and upon demand of the Solicitor, cannot produce or cannot give a good account of what has become of it, before one or two persons or the Attorney, he shall be judged guilty of the breach of the law, and to be accordingly dealt withal, and that the law shall extend to enquiry, especially to guns and other prohibitions, as powder, shot, lead, wine or liquors, that hath been merchandised, or conveyed away to the Indians, since the law made on that subject." And the people by general ticket, elected in May, 1650, William Dyre, Attorney General. Huge Burt, Solicitor do.

The same year, William Coddington embarked for England; and in 1651 obtained a Charter for Rhode-Island proper, and the Islands in the Narragansett Bay; Newport

and Portsmouth submitted to this government; Providence and Warwick, continued
under the old Charter. Afterwards, in the
same year, John Clark and Roger Williams
were dispatched to England, to obtain a
repeal of Coddington's Charter, and in 1652
it was revoked, on account of which, no
attorney and solicitor General's were elected in 1651–2.

1653.	John Easton,	Attorney General.
	—— ——	Solicitor do.
1654.	John Cranston,	Attorney General.
	—— ——	Solicitor do.
1655.	John Cranston,	Attorney General.
	John Greene,	Solicitor do.
1656.	John Easton,	Attorney General.
	Richard Bulgar,	Solicitor do.
1657.	John Greene, Jr.	Attorney General.
	James Rogers,	Solicitor do.
1658.	John Greene, Jr.	Attorney General.
	James Noyes,	Solicitor do.
1659.	John Greene,	Attorney General.
	—— ——	Solicitor do.
1660.	John Easton,	Attorney General.
	Richard Bulgar,	Solicitor **do.**

1661.	John Easton,	Attorney General.
	Peter Tadman,	Solicitor do.
1662.	John Easton,	Attorney General.
	Richard Bulgar,	Solicitor do.
1663.	John Sanford,	Attorney General.
	Richard Bulgar,	Solicitor do.
1664.	John Easton,	Attorney General.
	Lawrence Torner,	Solicitor do.
1665.	John Easton,	Attorney General.
	William Dyre,	Solicitor do.
1666.	John Easton,	Attorney General.
	William Dyre,	Solicitor do.
1667.	John Easton,	Attorney General.
	Edward Richmond,	Solicitor do.
1668.	John Easton,	Attorney General.
	William Dyre,	Solicitor do.
1669.	John Easton,	Attorney General.
	Edward Richmond,	Solicitor do.
1670.	John Sanford,	Attorney General
	Edward Richmond,	Solicitor do.
1671.	Joseph Torrey,	Attorney General
	William Harris,	Solicitor do.
1672.	John Easton,	Attorney General
	Edward Richmond,	Solicitor do.

2*

1673.	John Easton,	Attorney General.
	Robert Williams,	Solicitor do.
1674.	John Easton,	Attorney General.
	Robert Williams,	Solicitor do.
1675.	Weston Clarke,	Attorney General.
	Robert Williams,	Solicitor do.
1676.	Weston Clark,	Attorney General.
	Robert Williams,	Solicitor do.
1677.	Edward Richmond,	Attorney General.
	Robert Williams,	Solicitor do.
1678.	Edward Richmond,	Attorney General.
	Edmond Calverly,	Solicitor do.
1679.	Edward Richmond,	Attorney General.
	Edmond Calverly,	Solicitor do.
1680.	Weston Clarke,	Attorney General.
	Robert Williams,	Solicitor do.
1681.	Edmond Calverly,	Attorney General.
	———— ————	Solicitor do.
1682.	John Pococke,	Attorney General.
	Richmond Barnes,	Solicitor do.
1683.	Weston Clarke,	Attorney General.
	———— ————	Solicitor do.
1684.	John Pococke,	Attorney General.
	———— ————	Solicitor do.
1685.	Weston Clarke,	Attorney General.
	H. Brown,	Solicitor do.

1686. James Williams   Attorney General.

———— ————   Solicitor   do.

1687.   ⎧ Charter superceded by the
1688.   ⎨ appoinment of Sir Edmond Andros, as Governor of New-England.

1689.   ⎰ In May 1669, Charter resumed, and former officers re-established.

1690. John Pococke,   Attorney General.

1691. No record.

1692. No record.

1693. No record.

1694. No record.

1695. No record.

1696. John Smith,   Attorney General.

1697. No record.

1698. John Pococke,   Attorney General.

1699. John Pococke,   do.

1700. John Rhodes,   do.

1701. John Pococke,   do.

1702. Nathaniel Dyre.   do.

1703. Same,   do.

1704.	Joseph Sheffield,	Attorney General.
1705.	Same,	do.
1706.	Simon Smith,	do.
1707.	Same,	do.
1708.	Same,	do.
1709.	Same,	do.
1710.	Same,	do.
1711.	Same,	do.
1712.	William Coddington,	do.
1713.	John Hammett,	do.
1714.	Same,	do.
1715.	Weston Clarke,	do.
1716.	Same,	do.
1717.	Same,	do.
1718.	Same,	do.
1719.	Same,	do.
1720.	Same,	do.
1721.	Henry Bull,	do.
From May, 1721, to May, 1732,	Daniel Updike,	do.
From 1732, to 1741,	James Honyman, Jun.	do.

This year, the act appointing one Attorney General for the Colony was repealed, and an act passed, appointing Attornies for Counties.

1741. {
James Honyman, Jun., Attorney for the county of Newport.
William Walton, Attorney for the county of Providence.
Daniel Updike, Attorney for Kings, now Washington county.
}

1742. {
James Honyman, Jun., Attorney for the county of Newport.
John Andrews, Attorney for the county of Providence.
Daniel Updike, Attorney for the county of Kings.
}

This year, the act of 1741 was repealed, and the act appointing one Attorney General for the colony, revived.

From May, 1743, to June, 1757, } Daniel Updike, Attorney General.

From June, 1757, to May, 1766, } Augustus Johnson, Attorney General.

From May, 1766, to Sept. 1770, } Oliver Arnold, Attorney General.

From Oct. 1770, to May, 1777, } Henry Marchant, Attorney General.

From May, 1777, to May, 1787, } William Channing, Attorney General.

From May, 1787, to May, 1789, } Henry Goodwin, Attorney General.

1789.   David Howell,   Attorney General.

1790.   Daniel Updike,   do.

From May, 1791, } William Channing, Attorney
to Sept. 1793,   }   General.

From Oct. 1793, } Ray Green, Attorney General.
to May, 1798,   }

From May, 1798, } James Burrill, Jun., Attorney
to 1813,   }   General.

From 1813 } Samuel W. Bridgham, Attorney Gen-
to 1817, }   eral.

From 1817 } Henry Bowen, Attorney General.
to 1819, }

From 1819 } Dutee J. Pearce, Attorney General.
to 1825, }

From 1825 to the } Albert C. Greene, Attorney
present time,   }   General.

Up to the period when Mr. Bull was elected Attorney General, no materials or reminiscenses for
biographies of the Lawyers, who held those appointments, can now be obtained by the most diligent enquiries. The memoirs of the Attorney
Generals, commencing with Mr Bull, are given in
consecutive order, up to the time of Mr. Howell,
who has but recently deceased. Those who have
succeeded him, are now living, with the exception
of Mr. Burrill and Mr. Bridgham.

BIOGRAPHICAL SKETCHES.

HENRY BULL.

THE only history that is to be obtained of Mr. Bull, is extracted from a communication from Major Henry Bull, of Newport, recently deceased; a descendant of the subject of this memoir. Henry Bull, Esquire, one of the ancient Attorney Generals of this State, " was the son of Henry, who was the son of the Henry Bull who was one of the first pur-

South-Kingstown, but whether he was born there, or at Newport, cannot now be ascertained. He lost his father when he was about six years old, and his mother, sisters and brothers, within a few years after. He was, by his grandfather, committed to the care of his daughter Mary, widow of James Coggeshall. Soon after, his grandfather died, and his aunt Coggeshall brought him up. He was put to the carpenter's trade, at which he worked a few years after he came of age; during which time, he built the house where I now live. This house con-

tinued to be his residence, as long as he lived.—
The land on which it stands, he inherited from his
grandfather, and from whom the estate has regularly descended to me. He owned the Dumplin
farm, in Jamestown, and a farm in Narragansett,
besides a considerable landed estate in Newport."

"He married Martha Odlin; by whom he had
four sons and three daughters. His second wife,
was Phebe Coggeshall; by whom he had seven
sons and three daughters. His personal appearance was prepossessing—he was nearly six feet
high—light complexion and blue eyes—was well
proportioned and handsome; and in his manners
he was graceful. He was much celebrated for his
talents and wit. He had a good common education, for those days. I have heard," says Major
Bull, the aged, who had been acquainted with him,
relate what he had told them about his law education. " When he made up his mind to practice law,
he went into the garden, to exercise his talents in
addressing the court and jury. He then selected
five cabbages in one row, for Judges, and twelve in
another row, for Jurors—after trying his hand there
awhile, he went boldly into court, and took upon
himself the duties of an advocate, and a little observation and experience there, convinced him, that
the same cabbages were in the court house, which

he thought he had left in the garden ; five in one row, and twelve in another."

"But by whatever means, he acquired a knowledge of the law, he certainly rose to the height of his profession, as a practitioner in the courts of law and admiralty, as the profession stood in his day. He was one of that kind of men, whose *on-dits* were never forgotten, as long as the generation lasted, which was on the stage of life with him." '

"He was occasionally a member of the House of Representatives, from Newport : elected Attorney General in 1721,—re-elected in 1722, and declined serving. Daniel Updike was elected to fill the vacancy. He was elected Speaker of the House of Representatives, in 1728-9—was one of the committee to revise the colony laws in 1728—was one of the committee to conduct and manage the controversy, between the colonies of Rhode-Island and Massachusetts, respecting the eastern boundary.— He was Chief Justice of the Court of Common Pleas, at its first establishment, in 1749."

"He partook liberally of the enjoyments of life— was of an amiable and engaging disposition; and lived to a great age : having been born November 23d, 1687, and dying December 24th, 1771, aged 84."

3

It is in tradition from his associates in the profession, that Mr. Bull was very able in debate, and possessed strong native and intellectual energy— was quick to perceive, and ready to apply every incident, to the advantage of his cause. United with this native power, was the happy talent of amplification. Upon the whole, what resemblance existed, between the ancestor and his descendant, lately deceased, is left for others to determine.

JAMES HONYMAN

Was the son of the Reverend James Honyman, (Rector of Trinity Church, Newport, and Missionary from the society for the propagation of the Gospel in Foreign Parts, who entered upon the duties of his office in 1704, and died in 1750.) What were his literary attainments, and under whom he was educated, cannot now be ascertained; but it is to be inferred from the respectable standing, and the clerical acquirements of his father, that the subject of this memoir, was as highly instructed as

der whom he studied law, or at what period he was admitted to the bar, is equally uncertain; but his elevated standing in the profession, and his early promotion to the highest official stations in the Colony, warrant the conclusion that his legal education was regular and thorough.

In May, 1732, Mr. Honyman was elected Attorney General of the Colony, in the place of Daniel Updike, who in the political canvass of that year, declined a re-election, and stood as candidate for Governor. He was annually re-elected to the same office, until May, 1741, when the law appointing one Attorney General for the Colony, was repealed, and the act appointing County Attornies, was substituted. Under the last mentioned act, Mr. Honyman was elected King's Attorney, for the County of Newport, for the years 1741–2, when the act was repealed, and the former one, appointing one Attorney General for the Colony, was revived.

Mr. Honyman, was one of the committee on the Eastern boundary controversy, between Massachusetts and Rhode-Island; and one of the counsel, who argued the cause in behalf of Rhode-Island, before the commissioners appointed by the King, at Providence, in June, 1741: tradition speaks in the most respectful terms, of his forensick efforts, on that occasion. He was also one of the committee, appointed by the Legislature, to appeal from the judgment of the commissioners, and to prepare the documents, and draw up a history of the cause, to be laid before the King in council.

In 1756, Mr. Honyman was elected first Senator, in the Legislature of the Colony, and was successively re-elected to the same office, until May, 1764. In the January Session preceding, the General Assembly remonstrated in a decisive tone, against the increased rigors of the sugar act. The irritations of this and the other Colonies augmenting at the other acts and measures of the British Parliament; and Mr. Honyman feeling himself strongly attached to and favoring the views of the ministerial party, withdrew as a candidate for Senator, at the annual canvass in May; and Mr. Peleg Thurston was elected as his successor.

In 1755, Governor Hopkins, Mr. Honyman, and George Brown, were appointed by the General Assembly, commissioners to attend the Congress of Governors and Commissioners of the Northern Colonies, called by Lord Loudoun, to be holden at Boston, to concert measures to defeat the enemy.

Shortly after Mr. Honyman resigned his seat in the Senate, he was appointed by the Crown, Advocate General of the Court of Vice Admiralty in the Colony; which he continued to hold, discharging its duties to public satisfaction, until the Revolution. In February, 1776, the General Assembly passed a Vice Admiralty law; and appointed the officers under it. Hostilities having already commenced between the colonies and the Mother Country, and the public mind at this period, being highly excited, Mr. Honyman, at the June session following, appeared before the Legislature, and in the most respectful terms, represented the circumstances under which he held His Majesty's commission of Advocate General of the Court of Vice Admiralty. In a nervous and feeling address, he deplored the unhappy controversies

3*

that were tearing the two countries asunder, and expressed his desire to deliver up his commission, if the Assembly requested it. The Legislature, therefore, passed the following resolve· "That, James Honyman, Esquire, Advocate General in the Court of Vice Admiralty in this Colony, under the Crown of Great Britian, having appeared before, and informed this Assembly that if his holding said office be disagreeable to the Colony, he would deliver up his commission. *It is voted and resolved*, that his holding the same is disagreeable to this Colony, and that the sheriff of the county of Newport call upon the said James Honyman, to receive said commission, and that he deliver it to his Honor the Governor, to be lodged in the Secretary's office." The deportment of Mr. Honyman in this instance, feeling himself bound as he did, by his oath of allegiance, to the Crown, on the one hand, and conscientiously refusing to offend the feelings of his native state, on the other, reflects a rich lustre on the character of the christian, the gentleman, and the devoted lover of his country.

In December, 1776, the British took possession of the Island of Rhode-Island. On the 15th of January, 1778, while Newport was in their possesion, Mr. Honyman died, aged sixty seven years. He was interred in Trinity church on the side of the entrance by the north gate. The following inscription is on the stone which covers the grave.

SACRED TO THE MEMORY

of

JAMES HONYMAN, Esquire.

Eminent in his profession, as an Attorney at Law, and many years employed in the most important offices

OF

GOVERNMENT.

He died February 15th, 1778,

AGED 67 YEARS.

As a speaker, Mr. Honyman was elaborate, but his industry, talents and faithfulness, commanded an extensive and profitable practice, at Newport, and on the circuits. In deportment he was dignified—always dressed in the best fashions of the times—scrupulously formal in manners—domestic, yet social, in his habits. In person, he was tall, broad-shouldered and muscular, but not fleshy. He was severely afflicted and somewhat disfigured by a large wen, pendent from his jaw bone, "too large for extirpation."

Mr. Honyman married Elizabeth, the daughter of George Golding, a merchant of Newport; and left two sons and six daughters. His sons, George and John, died in early manhood. Mary, his eld-

est daughter was married to Mr. Brown; Elizabeth, to William Wanton, —————— ——————, to
Joseph Wanton, Jr., sons of Governor Wanton;
Catharine, to Mr. Tweedy; Susannah, to Abraham Redwood, Jun.; and Penelope, to the Rev.
George Bisset, rector of Trinity Church. Most of
his daughters and grand-daughters, having married British officers, or Americans adhering to the
cause of the Crown, departed with the enemy,
when the British evacuated Newport; and the
estates devised to them by Mr. Honyman, were
confiscated. After the Revolution, they petitioned
to the Legislature for restoration.

Upon the application, in behalf of the children,
of Joseph Wanton, Jun., in 1784, the committee
reported, "that from the documents to us produced, it appears, that the estate was confiscated
as the estate of Joseph Wanton, Jun., Esquire, but
that the said Joseph Wanton, Jun., never had the
fee of said estate, either in deed or possession; but
that the same belonged unto James Honyman, who
by his last will and testament, bearing date the
15th day of January, 1778, gave and devised the
same unto his three grandchildren, daughters of
the said Joseph Wanton, Jun., viz: Mary, Elizabeth and Ruth, who all married British officers;
and who are subjects of his Britanic Majesty, and
this State can have no claim on the same by way

of confiscation, it being in the heirs and devisees of the said James Honyman, who can hold the same," and the estate was accordingly surrendered and restored. At the October session of the General Assembly following, Mrs. Catherine Tweedy, and Mr. Abraham Redwood and wife, petitioned, with a like prayer, for restoration; stating, that the judgments by which said estates were confiscated, was rendered after the signature of the preliminaries of peace. At the succeding session the committee to whom said petition was referred, reported to the Legislature: " That the Superior Court of Judicature was held on the third day of March, 1783, the day on which hostilities ceased in America; and that the confiscation of said estate was made on the 7th of March ;" and the estate was restored to the petitioners. These are instances of hair breadth escapes from the penalties of the law, which no patriotic heart can regret. It may here be remarked, that every Rhode-Islander feels a pride in the reflection, that in no instance, after the revolutionary conflict was decided, did the Legislature refuse, upon application, to restore confiscated property, in their possession.

Of Mr. Honyman's family, no lineal descendants are remaining in this country ; and the estate acquired by his frugality and toil, has been alieniated long ago.

DANIEL UPDIKE.

His ancestors, were among the first settlers in Rhode-Island. One of them, by the maternal side, was "Richard Smith, Scu'r. who for his conscience to God, left fair possessions in Gloucestershire, in England, and adventured with his relations and estate to New-England, and was a most acceptable inhabitant and prime leading man in Taunton, Plymouth Colony. For his conscience sake, (many difficulties arising,) he left Taunton and came to the Narragansett country, where by God's mercy, and the favor of the Narragansett Sachems, he broke the ice, (at his great charge and hazard,) and put up in the thickest of the barbarians, the first English house among them." *

In 1664, when New Amsterdam, now New York, surrendered to the English, under Colonel Nichols, Gilbert Updike, a German physician of considerable celebrity, and his three brothers, Richard, Daniel and James emigrated to the Colony of Rhode-Island. Gilbert married the daughter of Richard Smith, and settled on his estate. In the great Cedar Swamp battle with the Indians in 1675, Rich-

---

*See Roger Williams' letter, Appendix, No. 1.

ard was killed, and Daniel and James dangerously wounded.* James afterwards died of apoplexy.— Daniel, on a voyage to Europe, was captured by the Algerines,† and ransomed by Major Richard

---

* Captains Johnson, Danforth, Gardner, Marshall and Seely, and Mr. Richard Updike, were among the slain, in the battle of 1675, and with the forty, were buried in one grave, in the south-east part of the garden of the Smith house, near Wickford. A tree, known as the "Grave Apple Tree," grew upon the grave, and was broken off in the September gale of 1815. But the stump now remains, which will designate the place. "State munificence has left uncovered, the remains of those devoted and conquering Forty, who spilt their life blood, in the great battle, for the salvation of the *whites*, against the tomahawk and scalping knife of the native Narragansetts.

> * * * * * * * * * * * * "pass not on
> Ere thou hast bless'd their memory, and paid
> Those hallowed tears which soothe the virtuous dead:
> O! *Stranger!* Stay thee, and the scene around
> Contemplate well; and if perchance thy home
> Salute thee with a father's honor'd name
> Go call thy sons—instruct them what a debt
> They owe their ancestry, and make them swear
> To pay it." * * * * * * *

† Letter from William Harris to his wife, dated "Algiers, April 6th, 1680. * * * * * * * Taken in a ship from Boston, bound to England, on the 24th of January, and they were all sold, in the Market on the 23d and 24th of February, and shut up till the last of March. John Chapman of Boston, promises 1200 dollars, William Harris,

Smith, Jr., with fifteen hundred gun locks. He afterwards died in England. Between the years 1665 and 1670, Mr. Richard Smith, sen'r. died, and devised to his son, Major Richard Smith, who had been a Major in Cromwell's service, and contributed to establish him as Protector, the greater part of his estate, and Major Smith dying in 1692 without issue, devised it mostly to his sister Updike.

The sons of Gilbert were Lodowick, Daniel and James. Lodowick only, survived his father, married Catharine, the daughter of Thomas Newton, and died in 1737, leaving Daniel and five daughters. (Richard, the eldest, having died before his

---

800 dollars and expenses to make out 1200. Mr. Leget's ransom cost him 5,000 dollars." In this letter he says, "since I came, I saw Daniel Updike, and he says he had a plague-sore, and that the said sickness is here every summer, and begins in May, and that the last summer here died 9 or 10 of the English captives, but some say not so many. Speak to Mr. Smith to redeem him and tell Lodowick, his brother, Mr. Smith, Mr. Brindley and others."

In another letter from William Harris to Mr. Brindley at Newport, dated April 4th, 1680, he says "pray tell Mr. Smith, Daniel Updike is well—He may do well to redeem him." ***************

From a copy of an incorrect manuscript in the possession of the late Moses Brown.

father, leaving two sons, Richard and the late John Updike of Providence.) Esther married Dr. Fosdick of New London. Sarah married Dr. Giles Goddard,* the father of the late William, and grandfather of the professor William G. Goddard. Abigail married Matthew Cooper, and Martha and Catharine died single at advanced ages. Daniel was educated in his father's house, by an able French instructor, in the Greek, Latin and French languages, and his sisters, in the Latin and French. After Daniel's education was completed, he visited Barbadoes, in the company of a friend of his father's; and was admitted to the first circles of society on the Island. His intercourse with the English residents was highly beneficial, in improving his mind, and polishing his manners. Upon his return, he immediately applied himself to the study of the law. After his admission he opened an office in Newport; married Sarah, the daughter of Governor Benedict Arnold, and she dying without issue, he married for his second wife, Anstis Jenkins, the grand-daughter of Mr. Wilkins, whose wife was a Polish lady, who by her intermarriage with Mr. Wilkins, below her degree, lost the favor of her family and emigrated with him to America. By this connexion, Mr.

---

* See Appendix, No. 2.

4

Updike became possessed of a considerable property, in addition to his patrimonial estate.

Mr. Updike continued in profitable practice, at Newport. From his popularity of manner and prompt discharge of official duty, he soon rose into public favor. In 1722, Henry Bull, Esq. having been elected Attorney General and declining the office, Mr. Updike was elected to fill the vacancy. He was annually re-elected by the suffrages of the people, until May, 1732, when he declined, having been nominated for Governor of the Colony, in opposition to Governor William Wanton. From Mr. Updike's general popularity, his success was expected; but during the canvass, an impression was industriously made, that if he succeeded, the titles to the estates by Fone's records, (then safely nailed up in a chest, by order of the Legislature of the Colony, and deposited in the Secretary's office,) in which he was a large claimant, would be re-opened, and the titles subsequently granted by the Legislature, of the same lands, jeoparded; he was consequently defeated.

In 1723, he was appointed, by the General Assembly, as State's counsel to attend the trial of the thirty-six pirates, captured by Capt. Solgar, commander of his Majesty's ship Greyhound, twenty-six of whom were executed at Newport in July of that year.*

An angry controversy had subsisted between the Colonies of Connecticut and Rhode-Island, respecting the boundary line between them. For the purpose of an amicable termination of it, in 1724, the Legislature of Rhode Island appointed a board of commissioners, of which Mr. Updike was one, to meet the commissioners of Connecticut, to effect an adjustment of this irritating subject. All efforts to procure a settlement, proved fruitless. It continued an open controversy until 1726, when it was finally decided by the King in Council.

The Eastern Indians were exasperated by the encroachments upon their territories, by the whites of Massachusetts, and were instigated to commence depredations, by the French missionaries from Canada. In 1724, the Colony of Massachusetts sent an expedition to subdue them, and demanded assistance from Connecticut and Rhode Island, effectually to prosecute the war. The General Assembly of Rhode-Island appointed a committee, to answer the letter of the Governor of Massachusetts, upon their demand; and to send an agent from

---

* Those who may be desirous to peruse this interesting and curious trial, see Appendix, No. 3.

this Colony to Canada. The following is the answer, as drafted bv Mr. Updike, one of the Committee.

"The General Assembly. having inspected into and considered the nature of the unhappy war between the Massachusetts Government and the Indian enemy, with its rise and progress, as also the various circumstances, that attend the same; do, upon the whole of what has been laid before them, conclude; that, although the said Indian rebels deserve nothing but a total extirpation for their continued and repeated rebellions, hostilities and perfidiousness, yet, it would be by no means justifiable in the Colony of Rhode-Island, to join with the Province of Massachusetts, in the prosecution of war, as things are at present circumstanced, and that for the following reasons."

"1st. The Colony of Rhode-Island, although small, is far extended upon the sea coast, and has a frontier to defend, and ward off the strokes of cruel and insulting enemies by sea, from the colonies of Massachusetts and Connecticut, which (considering the smallness of the colony, compared with those two great governments,) will be thought a due proportion of the general calamity of the Country, of this nature, were they exempted from contributing to defend against the enemy by land : For it is certain, that the people of the Colony of Rhode-Island are upon such occasions frequently alarmed, and have been exposed to very considerable charge, in fitting out vessels, in times of war and peace; the good effects whereof, the neighboring governments were made partakers. And therefore, it cannot be thought incumbent on this government, or for the good of the governments in general, that such a small colony, and so great a frontier, should be weakened

war, in an offensive manner, so foreign from their borders; and especially, when this colony, at this juncture, is carrying on, at its own charge, for the defence of the country, on said frontier, a fortification, the accomplishment whereof, will exceed ten thousand pounds."

" 2d. The Indian enemies were subjects of our sovereign lord, King George, and under his immediate protection, and in particular, under his government and dominion of Massachusetts. Wherefore, this government think, it would be unadvised in them, to join in the prosecution of said war, until his Majesty's pleasure was known upon the application, already made upon him: For this being an intestine war, happening in Massachusetts only, and a controversy of the King's subjects only, and that about property, who knows but that his Majesty, in his great wisdom, may find out and prescribe ways, to make those wild and inaccessible subjects of his,

4*

come in and tamely submit to his Government, without the melancholy prospect, we now have, of
shedding much blood—distressing and impoverish-
ing the whole land."

"3d. The Colony of Rhode-Island was never ad-
vised with, by the Province of Massachusetts, before
they involved themselves in this inextricable difficulty; nor did said Province ever concert measures
with this Colony, either in proclaiming war against
said Indians, or in any of their treaties they formerly had with them; then they generally took care
to restrict the trade with them to their own Province, if not to particular men. And shall this Colony, without the conjunction and united force of the
neighboring governments, on the continent, buy for
Massachusetts, this privilege, with the blood of
the young and strong?"

"Notwithstanding, the Colony of Rhode-Island
has a more tender regard for his Majesty's subjects
of the neighbouring governments, and more sincere
affection for his Majesty's interest, than to see his
subjects slaughtered and destroyed, his territories
depopulated and laid waste; and be guilty of su-
pine slothfulness, rejecting any reasonable application to them for succor and relief; for in case the
said war had been carried on in the defensive
manner, this Colony would, (if need had been,)
have lent all due assistance, until his Majesty's

pleasure had been known; but cannot think it justifiable in them to join in said war [since made offensive] until then."

" As respecting the proposition, of sending a man to Canada, from this Government,—it is the opinion of the General Assembly, that the same would create unnecessary charges. But they order and direct a letter be sent them from this government, by the messenger sent by Massachusetts, directed to Monsieur Voudriel, Governor thereof, to deter him and all those under the French government, from affording succor or encouragement to the Indian enemy; or for sheltering them after they have committed their depredations on the subjects of his British Majesty; and excite him to exert himself for the procuring an honorable peace with said Indians, for the ease and benefit of the English settlements; lest, by his Majesty's favor and permission, all the English governments on this continent of America unite their forces in ridding the whole land of this restless and lurking enemy, and all their abettors and encouragers.

Signed in behalf, and by order of the Assembly,
RICHARD WARD, *Recorder.*

At the August session of the Legislature, 1727, Mr. Updike was appointed one of the committe to draught an address, in behalf of the General Assembly, to be transmitted to George II. on his accession to the throne.

In 1729, Mr. Updike, William Jencks and Daniel Abbott, were appointed a committee to run the eastern line of Rhode-Island Colony with Massachusetts, according to the Charter; and as Attorney General, Mr. Updike was ordered to commence actions of ejectment against those claiming under Massachusetts, in order to try their titles.

It was enacted by the General Assemby, in 1731, that if Massachusetts appointed commissioners to settle the eastern line, the Rhode-Island commissioners were to meet them for that purpose; and if they should not agree, Richard Ward and Daniel Updike were appointed to draw a report of the case, and to represent the same to his Majesty for his decision thereon. In the autumn, of the same year, Rhode-Island proposed a reference for the purpose of settling the exciting controversy. If it should not be accepted, Mr. Updike and Mr. Martin were directed to prepare a full statement of the facts in dispute, for our agent in London, who was requested to lay the same before his Majesty. In May succeeding, Massachusetts accepted of the reference proposed by this Colony; but intending not to compromit their claims, selected Roger Wolcot, Ozias Pitkin and Joseph Fowler, of Connecticut, as their commissioners; and Rhode-Island, fearing that their recent controversy with Connecticut might have left unfavorable impressions on the minds of the commissioners thus selected, and

from mutual antipathies, long entertained, from which commissioners ought to be chosen to adjudicate upon their rights; and intending not to be defeated in this particular, Rhode-Island appointed

by Massachusetts, to determine this prolix controversy. New London was appointed as the place of meeting. The Rhode-Island commissioners and their counsel · attended; but those appointed by Massachusetts neglected, and no proceedings were had. At the autumn session of the Legislature, Rhode-Island appealed to his Majesty for the final determination of the question. In reward for the attendance of the commissioners, chosen by Rhode-Island, in endeavoring to bring this perplexing subject to an issue, the Legislature voted a present to each of them, of a silver tankard, of fifty pounds value.

In pursuance of the resolve of the Legislature, Governor Wanton, in behalf of the colony, in April, 1734, petitioned the King, to have this long controversy with Massachusetts, respecting the eastern line, settled. A committee of his Majesty's council, (May 10, 1738) reported, that such a case be left, by royal designation, to commissioners from out of the neighboring colonies. June 6th, 1739, Peter Bours, Daniel Updike, Godfrey Malbone and James Martin, addressed a communication to Massachusetts, mentioning that their agent in London had sent information of the King's pleasure, that commissioners should decide the question. It further proposed, as a means of preventing greater cost and altercation, that Rhode-Island and Massachusetts should each choose an equal number of plenipotentiaries to close the matter. By letter, under date of July 7th, 1739, Governor J. Belcher commissioned William Dudley, Benjamin Lynde, Jr., Nathaniel Hubbard, Samuel Wells and Thomas Graves, Esqrs., Thomas Cushing, Gentleman, and John Chandler, Esq., as the commissioners to settle the boundary question with Rhode-Island. The three first were of the Council; and the four last of the House. The commission provided, that if the parties could not agree, they should elect seven other commissioners, to make a final settlement, which was to be in writing, and handed to the commissioners of Rhode-Island and Massachusetts, before the 20th of November next. September 28th, 1739, the same commissioners, except J. Chandler, were appointed to inform their agent, Francis Wilks, in London, of what had passed at the interview of commissioners, of both Provinces, at Bristol.

The same seven commissioners as the first, on the 9th of October, 1739, were deputed to meet the Rhode-Island commissioners, and in case they should disagree, each body should select three referees from the adjacent governments.

Rhode-Island, at their December session of the Legislature, 1740, appointed Henry Bull, Daniel Updike, James Honyman, Jr., Peter Bours, Thomas Ward and Stephen Hopkins, to superintend and manage the affairs of the colony before the commissioners, appointed by the King, to hear and determine matters concerning the eastern boundary between Rhode-Island and Massachusetts; and prepare the necessary documents and papers; and also, to procure houses for the reception and entertainment of the commissioners. At the succeeding January session, the Governor and Council were requested to send a suitable vessel to Annapolis, to convey to Providence the commissioners appointed to sit on the trial, in such manner as should best comport with the dignity of the commissioners.

The Massachusetts legislature, in January, 1741, elected William Dudley, Samuel Wells, Benjamin Lynde, Jr. and Nathaniel Hubbard, of the Council, and Major Brown, Mr. Thomas Cushing, Colonel Chandler, Doctor Haile and Captain Watts, of the House, to lay their demands before his Majesty's commissioners, appointed to hear and decide upon

the aforesaid controversy, to whom, in the month
of March following, John Read and William Shirley, (afterwards Gov. Shirley) and in April, Job
Almy were added.*

In June, 1741, the King's commissioners met at
Providence, to hear and determine the cause.—
Cadwallader Colden, of New-York, was President
of the Board.   To Rhode-Island the issue was
eventful.   Her existence, as a colony, depended on
the decision.   If Massachusetts could establish her
claim to the Narragansett Bay, on the south-west,
the exclusive political jurisdiction of Rhode-Island
over the Narragansett waters would be lost forever; but if Rhode-Island could establish her jurisdiction over the territory described in her Charter,
she would hold, within her control, the great naval
and commercial key of New-England.   The land
was not a feather in the balance.   Both parties
were confident; and both were arrayed, with their
best talents, for the conflict.   Plymouth had become incorporated with Massachusetts, under the
corporate name of Massachusetts Bay, by which
she expected to succeed to every right and immu-
nity, attached to Plymouth, before the act of incorporation.   Each party thought they understood

---

* The proceedings of the Massachusetts legislature are
extracted from a communication from the Rev. Mr. Felt.

their case; they were ready for the trial; neither asked for postponement or delay. Mr. Shirley, or Bollan, and Auchmuty, distinguished advocates in Boston, argued the cause in behalf of Massachu-

of Rhode-Island. Judge Lightfoot, who heard the trial, spoke of it as one of the most anxious exhibitions that he ever witnessed, and that the argument of Mr. Updike, in the close, was a masterly effort. As Rhode-Island was the claimant, she was entitled to open the cause, and establish her claim.

1st. Her council exhibited the Royal Charter of 1663, to Rhode-Island, and claimed a line from the mouth of Seconk river, to extend three English miles, beyond the *ebbing and flowing* of the tide up Taunton river, as constituting the *head waters* of the Narragansett Bay ; and that this construction was warranted by the following words in the Charter : " Extending towards the east and eastwardly, three English miles, to the east and northeast of the most eastern or north-eastern *parts of the aforesaid Narragansett Bay,* as the said Bay lyeth and extendeth itself, *from the ocean* on the south or southwesterly, into the mouth of the river, which runneth towards the town of Providence, aud from thence, along the easterly side or bank of the said river, (higher called by the name of the

5

Seconk river) up to the falls, called Pawtucket falls, being the most northwesterly line of Plymouth Colony; and so from the said falls, in a straight line, due north, until it meets with the aforesaid line of the Massachusetts Colony."—Which construction, if adopted, would have carried the eastern bounds of Rhode-Island to near where the town of Taunton now stands, and would have excluded Massachusetts from any portion of the Narragansett Bay.

2d. That neither the letters patent to the Council of Plymouth, nor any authenticated copy of it, was produced; and that the recital of said deed, in the patent to Bradford and his associates, was not sufficient or legal evidence against the King's royal Charter to Rhode-Island.

3d. That the Plymouth letters patent contained no power to confer political jurisdiction, but only delegated power to grant property; and never having had any royal Charter conferring political jurisdiction, none was acquired over the territory designated in it. That the royal Charter to Rhode-Island gave political jurisdiction only, but not the right to meddle with property. Massachusetts, in answer to these objections, "professed that she had no apprehensions the controversy would turn, in the judgment of the commissioners, upon a point never before relied on, viz : That the colony of New Plymouth, having no charter from the Crown, the Rhode-Island charter must be the sole rule of determining the boundary, although the patent from the council of Plymouth, to Bradford and his associates, was prior to it. The colony of New Plymouth was a government *de facto*, and so considered by King Charles, in his letters and orders to them, before and after the grant of the Rhode-Island charter; and when the incorporation was made of New Plymouth with Massachusetts, &c., the natural and legal construction of the Province charter seems to be, that it should have relation to the time when the several governments, respectively incorporated, in fact, became governments."*

The judgment of the commissioners did not establish the claim of Rhode-Island to the extent demanded, but established a three mile line, from certain designated points, on the margin of the Narragansett Bay; although Mr. Colden, the President of the board, was in favor of fixing the line three miles from the point from whence the *tide ebbed and flowed* up Taunton river, in conformity to the views entertained by Rhode-Island.

Massachusetts expressed great surprise at the judgment of the commissioners; complained that

---

* Hutchinson.

the influence of the Councillor of New York, who was President, had too great a control at the board; and that the argument that had been too successfully made use of, in former controversies, had been revived, (that Massachusetts was too extensive, and that the other governments they were contending with, of which New-York was one, were too contracted.)

The adjudication gave to Rhode-Island the gore in controversy, called Attleborough gore, which was erected into a township, called Cumberland, after William, Duke of Cumberland, then just covered with the laurels gained at the battle of Culloden; Bristol entire; part of Swansea, being forty-seven families; and a great part of Barrington; which two last were constituted into a township, called Warren, in honor of Sir Peter Warren, Knight of the Bath, and Admiral in the Navy, an honest, benevolent gentleman, always favorable to trade; and the three mile strip, constituting the present towns of Tiverton and Little Compton.*

Judgment was rendered on June 30th, 1741, and the board adjourned to the 4th of September, that the colonies might affirm or appeal from their judgment. Massachusetts appealed to his Majesty in Council, from every part of the judgment, as griev-

---

* Douglass.

ous and injurious; and their committee were instructed to prepare all necessary documents for the Hon. Robert Auchmuty, and for Christopher Kelly, their agent in London, who was to be informed, that Mr. Auchmuty was associated with him, and would shortly depart, so that they might prosecute their appeal before the King in Council. At the October session of the Rhode-Island Legislature, Messrs. Updike, Honyman and Ward, were instructed to draw up a history of the whole cause, in order to be sent *home*, and funds furnished their agent to carry on the appeal.

In 1746, this protracted and bitter controversy was finally decided, by the King in Council, confirming the judgment of the commissioners; and the line was immediately run, and established in conformity to the decree.

The settling of this line cost each government about £4000, old tenor. Six shillings, sterling, per day, were allowed the commissioners each, and all charges in coming to, staying at, and returning from, the Congress.

The General Assembly of this colony allowed to their Attornies, before the commissioners, the following sums: To Daniel Updike, £125—James Honyman, £125—Peter Bours, £110—Thomas Ward, £125—Henry Bull, £80—Stephen Hopkins, £73.10.   5*

The General Assembly, at their December session, 1748, passed the following law · " That there be, by the General Assembly, annually, at their session holden on the first Monday of May, chosen and appointed one Attorney General for each county, who is hereby empowered to act and manage in all affairs, within the said county, for which he is elected, in as full and as extensive a manner as the Attorney General of this colony hath been accustomed to do; and that the act for choosing one Attorney General for the colony, be, and it is hereby declared null and void."

In May, 1741, James Honyman, Jr. was appointed Attorney General, for Newport county; William Walton, do. for Providence county; Daniel Updike, do. for Kings county.

In May, 1742, Mr. Updike was re-elected for Kings county, and also elected one of the committee to revise the laws. In May, 1743, the General Assembly having repealed the law relating to the appointment of Attorney Generals for counties, revived the former law, appointing one Attorney General for the colony, Mr. Updike was elected Attorney General; which office he continued to sustain, by annual re-elections by the people, until his death.

In 1745, the profession held their first bar meeting in this colony. The name of Mr. Updike appears first on the compact.*

In 1749, the Supreme Court decided, in a cause before them, that the statutes of England were not in force in this country, except they were introduced by statute. A decision, which shook the colony to its foundation. Messrs. Updike, Honeyman, John Aplin and Matthew Robinson, Attornies at Law, represented unto the General Assembly, by memorial under their hands, "that the Supreme Court in this colony, have, of late, judicially determined that the statutes of that part of Great Britain, formerly called England, are not in force in this government, except such as are introduced by some law of the colony. And this, notwithstanding all time heretofore, the courts throughout this colony, both superior and inferior, have admitted such statute as relate to the common law, to to be in force here, and have adjudged upon them as such, so that there has been no occasion of an act of the Assembly, for the formal introduction of those statutes. But as the case now stands, the laws of this colony are altogether imperfect, and scarcely any one law proceeding can now be commenced or brought to issue. And now, the Assembly having taken the same into consideration, *Re-*

---

* See compact, in Appendix, No. 4.

solved, that the memorialists be constituted a committee, to prepare a bill for introducing into this colony, such of the laws of England, as are agreeable to the Constitution."

The committee, at the next February session, made the following report:

"We, the subscribers, being appointed to report what statutes of Great Britain are, and ought to be in force in this colony, do report the following, viz:

The statutes of
Merton, concerning Dower.
Westminster, the first, as far as concerns bail.
Gloucester
Westminster. the second, *de donis conditionalibus*.
First, Henry V., chap. 5, of adtions.
Partition, in General.
Thirty-second of Henry VIII., concerning leases, saving and excepting the last paragraph of said statute.
Twenty-first of James I., chap. 16th, for limiting real actions, and that of the thirty-second of Henry VIII., chap. 2.
James and Elizabeth, and all other statutes that concern Bastardy, so far as applicable to the constitution of this colony.

All statutes against criminal offenders, so far as they are descriptive of the crime, and where the law of the colony hath not described, or enjoined the punishment also, always saving and excepting such statutes, as from the nature of the offences mentioned in them, are confined to Great Britain only.

The statute of the twenth-seventh, Henry VIII., commonly called the statute of Uses.

The statute of the twenty-ninth of Charles II., chapter 3d, commonly called the statute of Frauds and Perjuries.

The statutes of the twenty-second and twenty-third of Charles II., chap. 10th, for distributing the estates of intestates.

The statute of the third and fourth of William and Mary, chap. 14th.

The statutes of the fourth and fifth of Anne, chap. 16, relating to joint tenants and tenants in common.

That part of the statute of the ——— of Anne, that subjects lessees who hold over their term, against the will of the lessor, to the payment of double rent, during the time they hold over.

All statutes relating to the poor, and relating to masters and apprentices, so far as they are applicable in this colony, and where we have no law of the colony.   DANIEL UPDIKE,
                                       J. HONYMAN, Jr.,
                                       JOHN APLIN."

" And this General Assembly having taken the said report into consideration : *Do vote and resolve,* that all and every of the statutes aforesaid be, and and they are hereby introduced, into this colony, and shall be in force therein, until the General Assembly shall order otherwise."

The defeat of Gen. Braddock opened the American frontier to the savages, and their bloody incursions were made in all directions. In the year 1755, Gov. Hopkins and Mr. Updike were appointed by the legislature, commissioners in behalf of

---

Mr. Updike was Attorney General in 1751, on the trial of Thomas Carter, for the murder of William Jackson. The tragic circumstances under which the homicide was committed, and at a time when crimes of such enormity were rare, awakened the sympathy of the whole continent, and even reached the mother country. The deep interest it created, tradition has detailed in all its minuteness. Carter owned a small vessel, of which he went master, and sailed from Newport, where he resided, to New York. He was wrecked on Long Island, and lost all, and borrowed money to defray the expenses of his return. He landed on the Connecticut shore, and on his journey home, on foot, he fell in company with Mr. Jackson, a Virginian, bound to Newport, driving a horse laden with dressed deer skins, for sale, and the proceeds to be invested in Narragansett horses, for the home market. He was dressed in wash-leather small clothes,

this colony, to meet with his Excellency Major General Shirley, commander-in-chief of his Majesty's forces in America, to concert measures more effectually to prosecute the campaign against the French, in Canada.

---

snuff-colored jacket and red duffil over coat, a saw backed hanger at his side, and a watch with a green ribbon for a chain. Both being destined for the same place, they travelled together, passing New London late at night. On the 31st of December, 1750, they arrived at South Kingstown, and tarried at Nathan Nash's· The next morning, Carter complained of indisposition, and did not rise until noon. In the mean time, Jackson was anxious to depart, that they might reach Newport before night. Uususpicious of Carter's intention, Jackson delayed his departure, at his solicitation; procured Nash to shave him and cut his hair. Nash's wife observed, at the time, a particular black spot differing from his other hair, and saw some linen, marked W. I., and at Jackson's request, sewed some buttons on his overcoat, with untwisted thread. He showed a bag of money, weighing five or six pounds. In the afternoon they left. Carter procrastinated the journey by stopping at every shop and tavern on the way, and calling for liquor freely, until evening, assuring Jackson that there was time enough to reach the ferry, and take the earliest boat for Newport, in the morning. When passing the hill above where the Quaker's meeting house now stands, Carter stated it was too late to reach the ferry, before all were abed, and no admission could be obtained, and persuaded him to remain in an untenanted

In 1730, the first literary institution in the colony was formed, out of which subsequently grew the Redwood Library. Mr. Updike was one of its founders, and owned a considerable many shares in it. He was the first signer to the constitution

---

house, by the road,—the remains of the chimney are now observable. Jackson was still unsuspicious of any design or evil intention, and consented. But the loneliness of the deserted house, inspired him with uneasiness, he began to reflect on the circumstances which had passed, and complained to Carter, that all things did not appear right,—that he could not sleep, and insisted on proceeding. Carter tried to dissipate his fears, but it availed nothing. He insisted on proceeding, and when they left the house, Carter struck him with a stone, and felled him to the ground; Jackson begged for life, but Carter seized Jackson's hanger, and dispatched him. After rifling him, he took the dead body, weltering in blood, on his shoulder, and carried it near a mile, and deposited it under the ice, in the southern arm of the Petasquamscut river, and in cutting the hole he broke the hanger. On his return he concealed the great coat in the wall; covered with snow all appearances of the murder, and proceeded to Newport with the plunder. He slept at the ferry-house the remainder of the night; but fearing some evidences of the foul deed might be seen, and effectually to conceal all the appearances of the catastrophe, he early in the morning returned. On his arrival, a hunter, by the name of Jonathan Hazzard, being on an excursion, was near the spot.— The dogs scented the blood, and yelled furiously. Haz-

of the literary society ; and himself, Scott, Callender, Honyman, Ellery, and Checkley, were among
its most active and zealous members. From the
intimacy of these intelligent gentlemen with Dean
Berkely, who then resided in Newport, the utili-

---

zard enquired of the stranger what blood that could be ?
Carter replied it must be the blood of some deer. Hazard said there were no deer in that part of the country.
Carter became enraged, and ordered him to call off his
dogs and pursue his course, or he would meet with trouble.
Hazard being afraid of the man, from his appearance, did
so. Carter returned to the ferry, made some idle excuse
for his absence—exhibited great uneasiness—and hurried
to Newport. Although he had time enough to escape, he
was the earliest every morning at the ferry wharf to enquire, " What news from Narragansett ?" On the 22d of
February, about seven weeks after the murder, the body
was found by some fishermen ; yet Carter had never attempted to fly. On the 23d he was arrested : some of the
deer-skins—watch chain, and linen, marked W. I., were
found in his possession. He was examined ; but denied
all the circumstances—was committed and tried in April,
1751. Twenty-seven witnesses were examined against
him, which elicited all the facts before stated. Conscious
of his guilt, and expecting to be convicted, he had prepared his mind for the verdict, and heard it pronounced without any apparent emotion ; not even a muscle was moved.
But the additional sentence changed the whole scene. It
was the law then, that if the criminal was guilty of an ag-

ty of such a society, for the promotion of knowledge and science, was suggested. The learned
Dean sometimes encouraged and stimulated their
efforts by his presence. Mr. Updike and Dean
Berkely were intimate friends, and repeatedly visited Narragansett together; and the latter was so
much enraptured with the romantic prospect that
Barber's heights, in North Kingstown, exhibited, he
observed, that if the funds appropriated for Ber-
muda could be obtained, he would select it as the
most eligible site for his intended University. If
such an event had occurred, how different might
have been the literary character of Narragansett,
from what it now is? In testimony of the friend-

---

gravated homicide, or one without palliating circumstances, the court might add to the ordinary sentence, that the
body of the executed should be hung in chains. For this
he was not prepared ; and when it was announced from
the bench, he lost all self-possession—became entirely un-
nerved, and cried out for mercy from the gibbet ; exclaim-
ing it was too hard. He was executed May 10, 1751;
and his body was suspended from an iron frame, until his
flesh and bones fell from it. The creaking of the frame,
when waved by the wind, so terrified the people in those
superstitious days, that they dare not pass it in the dark.
An immense concourse of people attended the execution ;
and so many left Newport, that those who remained were
fearful of an insurrection of the slave population, and de-
spatched messengers for their return.

ship and esteem which the Dean entertained for Mr. Updike, he presented him, on his departure for Europe, an elegantly wrought silver coffee-pot; and after his arrival, sent him his "Minute Philosopher," which now remain in the family, as remembrancers of this distinguished divine.

Mr. Updike, in person, was about five feet, ten inches in height, with prominent features. As an advocate, he sustained a high reputation, and among other personal advantages, possessed a clear, full and musical voice. Dr. Bradford used to speak of him as being a "fine speaker, with great pathos and piercing irony." Among his professional brethren he was highly respected, and in all literary and professional associations of his time, his name stands at the head. His professioual acquaintances were extensive without the colony. His intimacy with Gridley, the colonial Attorney of Massachusetts, Shirley, who was appointed Governor by the Crown, and received his commission while attending the trial of the eastern boundary line, at Providence, Judge Auchmuty, the elder, and Bollan, induced him frequently to visit Boston. The two last named gentleman often argued causes in this colony, and occasionally made Mr. Updike's mansion their place of residence.

Mr. Updike possessed a large library in classical and general literature, a considerable portion of which is now extant.

In May, 1757, Mr. Updike was re-elected Attorney General; and died in the same month, having been elected by the people twenty-four years, Attorney General of the colony, and two years, Attorney General for the county of Kings. The General Assembly, at their June session ensuing, appointed Augustus Johnson to fill the vacancy.

From the records of St. Paul's church, under the rectorship of Dr. McSparran, the following entry is extracted,—" Colonel Updike of North Kings-town, Attorney General of the colony, died on Saturday, the 15th of May, 1757, about noon, and after a funeral discourse was preached by Dr. McSparran, was interred in the burial ground of the family, beside the remains of his father and second wife, Anstis Jenkins, mother of Lodowick and Mary Updike, his surviving children."*

---

* " May 2d, 1730, Daniel Updike, Attorney General of the colony, and Lieutenant Colonel of the militia of the islands in said colony, was baptized by the Rev. Mr. McSparran, by immersion, (in Petiquamscut river) in presence of Mr. McSparran, Hannah McSparran, his wife, and Josiah Arnold, Church Warden, as his witnesses."

McSparran's Church Records.

AUGUSTUS JOHNSON.

Mr. Johnson was born at Amboy, in New Jersey, about the year 1730. His mother was the daughter of Mr. Lucas, a French Huguenot. He was quite a child when his father died, and was entrusted to the care of an elder sister. He received a liberal, though not a collegiate education, in the state of New York. He came to Rhode-Island, when quite young, studied law with Matthew Robinson, Esq., who was his step-father, and settled in Newport. After a few years practice, he was considered one of the best lawyers in the state. But little positive information can now be obtained of his professional career. Time has thrown the veil of oblivion upon the causes in which he was engaged; and thus, for the most part, obscured the talent employed in them. Tradition speaks of him as a man of extraordinary powers in his particular calling, yet cannot point to the prominent cases in which his reputation was acquired. He had an unlimited confidence in his own ability, and would acknowledge no superior. He was equally ready in the office, or before the court. With an acute and penetrating mind, he could unravel the most

6*

intricate cases with apparent ease; but his great
forte was in sifting and reconciling discordant
testimony.   No matter how numerous the witnesses, or how misty their statements; no matter
how much time or space the scene covered; he
would divest the case of all extraneous circumstances, with such readiness, and present the prominent and material points with such clearness and
force, that the jury was impressed strongly in his
favor.   His great confidence in his own powers was
often mistaken, by the triors, for confidence in the
cause in which he was engaged.

Mr. Updike died in May, 1757, about a week after his twenty-sixth election to the office of Attorney General.   At the succeeding session, the General Assembly appointed Mr. Johnson to supply
the vacancy occasioned by his decease.   Mr. Johnson, by successive re-elections, held the office for
the term of nine years.   He was then, on account
of his strong adherence to the Crown, dropped by
the party which had formerly supported him.

Mr. Johnson was a man of singular firmness, and
was but little affected by the opinions of others.
The more sternly he was opposed by his political
enemies, the more firmly did he cling to his political opinions.   He had ever been a zealous royalist.
He considered it his duty to be so.   He saw public
opinion changing, but his views were unaltered.

He soon found himself in a minority; but it only made him the more zealous. He saw his best friends deserting him; but he seemed to feel a pride in stemming the torrent of public opinion; yet he expressed great regard for the state and people of Rhode-Island.

In the year 1765, in the height of popular excitement, he accepted the office of Stamp-master. His friends, who were yet left, endeavored to persuade him to resign it; others threatened him with violence, if he should dare to exercise its functions; but threats and persuasions were, by him, alike unheeded. He was constantly hissed at, and insulted in the streets; but it had little or no effect on his determinations. Some time in the autumn of 1765, his house was surrounded by an infuriated collection of men, who by their unusual tumult and rage, first led him to feel that his person was in danger. He retreated to his cellar, and was there secreted, until the mob had dispersed, and then left it in disguise. He was afterwards seized, and after suffering many indignities, a promise was extorted from him, to resign the office, with which he reluctantly complied.

In 1766, the stamp act was repealed. As soon as the news was received, the people of Newport erected a gallows, near the State House, and had the effigies of Mr. Johnson, Martin Howard, Jun., and Doctor Moffat, the Stamp-masters, conveyed through the streets, in a cart, with halters about their necks. They were carried to the gallows and hanged; and shortly after cut down and burned, amid the shouts and acclamations of the assembly. The popular indignation made it necessary for Mr. Johnson to seek protection on board of a British armed vessel, then lying in the harbor.

During the occupation of Newport, by the British, he held several civil appointments under the crown; and on the evacuation, at the close of the year 1779, he accompanied the enemy's forces to New York.

His property, in Newport, was confiscated; and as a remuneration for his persecutions, he received a pension from the British government as long as he lived; and after him the same was continued to his widow. who survived him many years. He left one son and three daughters; one of the latter is now living. His son, the late Major Matthew Robinson Johnson, served in the British army until the peace of 1800, when he disposed of his commission, and returned to his native country, and died a few years since. His widow now lives in the town of Johnson, which town, in 1759, was divided from Providence, and in compliment to the Attorney General, was named after him. At the time of his death he held the office of Judge of Vice-Admiralty, for the southern district of North America.

There are some men justly celebrated in their own day, who, on account of their peculiar sphere of action, lose that celebrity when their cotemporaries pass away. Thus it was with Augustus Johnson. Had his powers of intellect been turned to something, on which posterity could have fixed their attention, his name would now have been familiar to every son of Rhode-Island. But such were his employments, that nothing can now be learned of his character, but from tradition. Alas, for the reputation of that man, whose traditionary character is handed down by political opponents. He was an officer under the British Crown; he was opposed to the revolution;—what then can we expect would be his reputation, if seen only through the medium of strong political excitement?

OLIVER ARNOLD,

Was the son of Israel, and the grandson of John Arnold, a descendant of Richard, who was one of the Council of Sir Edmond Andros, in 1685; and a near relative of Benedict Arnold, President of the colony of Rhode-Island, prior to the appointment of Coddington, the first Governor. In boyhood he evinced a strong propensity for study, and an ardent thirst for knowledge. To gratify this ruling inclination, his father placed him with Dr. Webb, of Uxbridge, Massachusetts, a presbyterian clergyman of reputation and talent. Under his instruction and direction, he increased those habits of study and application, which were so eminently serviceable to him in after life. The father of Oliver was a wealthy landholder, and was much engaged in public business. With whom Oliver studied his profession, or in what year he was admitted to the bar, is not known. That he possessed a strong, elastic mind, with much early professioual talent, is shown by the anecdote related by the late Levi Lincoln, to the late Dr. Willard, of Uxbridge. "When at the bar," observed Lincoln, "a cause of considerable interest was entrusted to me; and on retainer, I was informed, by my client, that I should be opposed only by a young man, by the name of Arnold, from Glocester, Rhode-Island. Not expecting much display of talent from any one in that region, I was slovenly prepared for arguing the case; nor was my caution increased by the appearance of my antagonist—a tall, green-looking youth, who awkwardly seating himself at the bar, impressed me that I had nothing but a stripling to contend with. I made my speech with very little expectation of being answered; and conducted my argument throughout, with less skill and arrangement than usual, and awaited the reply of my youthful opponent. But what was my amazement," he continued, "to see him rise with the most perfect self-possession, and state his defence, and argue his cause, with an ability that would have done honor to Temple bar. He went on calmly, leading the reason of the jury and audience captive, and leaving myself in the back ground, as far as I confidently expected to have left him."— This trial spread the reputation of Mr. Arnold, as an advocate, far and wide. And from steady application and diligence, he soon rose to distinction in his profession, as a faithful and popular lawyer.

Mr. Arnold was born in Glocester, in 1726 In 1754 he married Elizabeth, the daughter of Daniel Brown, of Sandisfield, Massachusetts, the sister of the late Col. John Brown, who commanded a regiment under Gen. Benedict Arnold, at the

siege of Quebec—assisted in the capture of Ticon-
deroga—and in the successful battle on lake Cham-
plain.   He fell on Palatine plain, in defending Al-
bany against a party of Canadians and Indians.

For the greater convenience of practice, Mr. Arnold, in 1762, moved from Glocester to Providence,
and purchased an estate on North-main street, opposite the residence of the late Gen. Bridgham,
and continued constantly and indefatigably, engaged in his profession, in and out of the state.

Previous to his removal, he found time for the
cultivation of his talent for music.   His hours of
relaxation were devoted to practice on the violin,
on which he was a tasteful performer.   Tradition
still speaks of him, in the vicinity of his former residence, as a promoter of innocent festivity; often
carrying his violin, on his rural visits, for the encouragement of youthful recreation.   From the increased professional demands upon his time, he
was obliged, on his removal, to dispense with this
somewhat peculiar gratification.   Still his taste for
music and dancing continued, and so desirous was
he to have his daughters excel in this elegant and
fascinating amusement, that he engaged an Italian
performer to instruct them regularly at his own
house.

In May, 1766, Mr. Arnold was elected Attorney

General of the colony, as the successor of Augustus Johnson, who resigned in consequence of the agitations respecting the stamp act; under which he was one of the commissioners appointed by the Crown. Mr. Arnold was continued in the office by successive re-elections, by the people, until his death. During his practice, an unfortunate and acrimonious professional controversy arose between himself and John Aplin, Esq., a lawyer, in the same county. During its continuance, Mr. Aplin was prosecuted for official malpractice, and Mr. Arnold was employed to conduct the cause. In the ruin that was overwhelming his persecutor, Mr. Arnold anticipated more than a just retribution for any injuries done to himself; and it was then, for the first time, that he felt he could forgive him. He felt a strong antipathy to Mr. Aplin, knowing him to be his enemy. Personal feeling and resentment might, unknown to himself, mingle with his zeal in the course of justice. He made an ineffectual attempt to avoid the prosecution, and endeavoured to escape the necessity of a discharge of the duty which official obligation imposed upon him; but personal solicitation was urgent, and he was made to believe, that refusal was dereliction of the obligations officially enjoined upon him. It is to be regretted, that under these circumstances, he yielded to the demands of pretended professional duty, however zealously or speciously urged.

7

After hearing the testimony, and the defence by Mr. Aplin himself, which, according to tradition, was the most able and eloquent he ever made, Arnold summed up in reply. It was a maxim of his to perform, whatever he undertook, thoroughly. He did not shrink when actually engaged. The ability and power displayed by the Attorney General, on that occasion, was long remembered by one of the most attentive and crowded audiences ever collected in the court room. This trial resulted in a verdict against Aplin; and he immediately fled from the state, and, subsequently, was expelled from the bar. The merits of this case are stated, at large, in the memoirs of Aplin, and are therefore omitted here. It is sufficient to state, that this acrimonious controversy, and its consequences, embittered the remaining days of both parties. Arnold's opponent was crushed, and completely so; and it was his hand that dealt the annihilating blow, and drove his competitor a "houseless wanderer" from his family and his country, to seek an asylum in another clime. But the painful apprehension of Arnold, that under the circumstances, he might have done more than his duty, stung his conscience, and preyed upon his feelings for the rest of his life. It is due to truth to state, that between their immediate families, a subsequent intimacy existed until the grave closed over them.

Mr. Arnold was engaged in two important state

trials, during the period of his Attorney General-
ship. In addition to the feeling created by the
homicide involved in it, the trial of Carless and
others, excited an intense interest growing out of
the exasperated state of animosity existing between this country and Great Britain, respecting
the Stamp act. It arose from an affray which
took place on the third of May, 1768, in Newport,
between some of the citizens and Charles Carless
and others, officers of the Senegal, man-of-war,
then lying in the harbor. Carless, in his defence,
thrust his sword into the breast of one Henry
Sparker, which caused immediate death. Carless
and his associates were arrested, and tried at a
court, specially convened, in June, for that purpose,
—and after a full trial, they were acquitted; as
was also one Inman, for the supposed murder of
Foster; and others, arrested for crimes of less magnitude. These trials were conducted with a credit-
able ability by the Attorney General

His civil duties on the various committees, raised by the Legislature, on which the government
Attornies were usually appointed, and especially
on the one to compile the digest of 1787, were performed with ability.

The manner of Mr. Arnold was graceful and
easy. His countenance, when in a state of repose,
indicated nothing striking; but when excited by

argument, or when his feelings were aroused, he possessed uncommon attraction. He was a severe student; and was master of the few books that constituted a lawyer's library at that period. He was remarkable for the great retentiveness of his memory. What he once learned, he is said never to have forgotten ; and could repeat his authorities *verbatim*. He once repeated several passages, to fortify the position he had assumed, in the argument of a cause, the correctness of which was strenuously denied, and as positively reasserted. The court, for the due settlement of the controverted question, desired that the authorities might be produced. The demand was acceded to, and the quotation proved to be correct, to the letter. So effectually could he abstract his mind, that he could study "Coke upon Lyttleton" by the family fireside, or amid the discursive argumentations of a tavern bar-room, with perfect composure.

The character of Mr. Arnold has been handed down to us, as a lawyer of candor, probity and great uprightness; rejecting those mean and paltry cases which so often disgrace those who espouse them. But when engaged in a cause which his conscience approved, nothing could turn him in his course, or stay his exertion. The general impression of the probity of his character obtained for him, with court and jury, an influence, which every honest lawyer ought to possess. Loud and angry retort, or bitter sarcasm, were unknown to him. This, in no small degree, contributed to that professional respect of which he was so eminently deserving.

Mr. Arnold took a warm and active interest in the advancement of general education; and was a devoted patron of literary institutions. He was one of the council, before the legislature, to obtain the charter of Rhode-Island college, now Brown University; and contributed to its funds with a liberality commensurate with his circumstances; and ardently interested himself in promoting its prosperity.

Of the personal friends of Mr. Arnold, Mr. Alexander Campbell, of East Greenwich, was one to whom he was intimately attached. His death, which occurred suddenly, in 1769, the year before that of Mr. Arnold, deeply and seriously affected his feelings. Judge Bowler, Gov. Bradford, Matthew Robinson and Henry Marchant, were his warm friends and intimate associates, though some of them were his seniors in the profession.

Short, though flattering, was the career Mr. Arnold was destined to run. At the age of thirty-five —in the midst of his days and usefulness—death suddenly summoned him away. He died while at-

tending court in Washington county, at its October term, 1779, after a few days illness. Rejecting
the services of the less informed physicians, in the
neighborhood, Dr. Hunter, of Newport was called,
who unfortunately mistook his case, which if not
the immediate cause, materially hastened his dissolution. The court, then sitting, suspended business;
and a general gloom was spread over the village,
where he was well known and greatly respected.
Most of the citizens joined in the procession, to
render their last honors, and to mingle their re-
grets with the mournful cavalcade assembled to
convey his remains to Providence, where he was
interred, with the respect due to his talents, his
services to the state, and above all, to his unsullied
reputation.

Mrs. Arnold survived her husband twenty-nine
years, and departed this life in 1799. Of the three
children, Waity, Alfred and Mary—the latter is
still living. Alfred left three children at his decease. Mrs. Catharine R. Williams, the author-
ess, is the only surviving grandchild.

But little is known respecting the religious
state of Mr. Arnold's mind. Among his papers
were found these words: " A christian may triumph
in the death of Christ." It is inscribed on the slab

that is erected to his memory, in the north burial
ground, in Providence.

> "O! death where is thy sting?
> "O! grave where is thy victory? O! Hell where is thy terror?

> Oh, my soul! where are thine accusers?
> "Riches are but dust.   Honors are shadows.
> "Pleasures are bubbles, and man a lump of vanity,
> Compounded of sin and misery."

IN MEMORY

OF

OLIVER ARNOLD,

ATTORNEY GENERAL OF THIS COLONY.

A gentleman descended from an ancient and honorable
family.   But his principal renown was the fruit of
his Genius and indefatigable industry.   His
abilities and accomplishments were equal
to any station and character in life.
LIVING,
He fully acquired the love of his country ; and dying,
she dropped the unavailing tear.
HE DIED ON THE 9TH OF OCTOBER, 1770.
in the 35th year of his age.

The following lines, "on the death of Oliver
Arnold, Attorney General of the Colony, and Bar-
rister at Law," were inserted in the Providence
Gazette.

> Hail man beloved! O worthy Arnold hail,
> Forgive the tears, that loss of thee bewail,
> Ah! peaceful thought, that thou shall bless no more

Those thou didst bless, and greatly bless before.
But now the scene is changed and the short span
Of life is closed, the fleeting life of man,
The seraph genius, the exalted mind
Has fled to seats of happiness divine.
The angel, scattering death through all the host,
Hath snatched away our friend, our pride, our boast,
Arnold hath lived, but now his life is done,
So good, and yet, alas! so short 'tis spun,
With virtue, learning, wit and worth combined,
Benev'lence warmed his breast and fired his mind:
Unmoved by prejudice, unbribed by gold;
Justice he sought, in conscious virtue bold;
Still friendly to the good, his opening door
Revived, supplied, and e'er relieved the poor.
And while around his benefits he spread,
Vice he restrained, and for the needy *plead:*
Through science's flowery paths, with ease he went,
And liberal knowledge ope'd his stores and lent—
Of that blest treasure, that exalts the mind,
Rendering it lofty, noble and refined.
Correct with spirit, eloquent with ease,
Intent to reason and polite to please,
Persuasive eloquence sat upon his tongue,
While he "the right approved, condemned the wrong."
Through all the varied scenes of life approved,
He as a father, friend and Husband loved.
But now no more, his soul has winged its way
Up to the regions of Eternal day.

From the same paper the following is extracted:

October 13th, 1770. Died, Oliver Arnold, at South
Kingtown, aged 34, Attorney General—native of Glocester
—descended from Gov. Benedict Arnold—admitted to the
bar at the age of 25—elected Attorney General at the age
of 28. His genius was lively and active—his ideas extensive and beautifully arranged—his conceptions were quick,

clear, and radiant—his judgment sound. In his writings, his style was manly, pure and correct. In his pleadings at the bar, his language was nervous and expressive, his elocution, harmonious, graceful, pathetic; and in the course of his extensive business, he fully sustained the best of characters, that of an honest man. In him, the rights and liberties of America, lost a steady and firm friend—the colony a faithful officer—the town of Providence one of her most useful and worthy citizens.

HENRY MARCHANT,

Was born at Martha's Vineyard, in the colony of Massachusetts, in April, 1741. His father, Hexford Marchant, was a captain in the merchant's service; his wife was a Butler. She died when the subject of this memoir was four years old, and a short time after the removal of the family to Newport. Captain Marchant married, for his second wife, the daughter of the first, and sister of the second Gov. Ward. At the age of eight years, Henry had the misfortune to lose his father, who died in the West Indies, in the employment of Henry Collins, then one of the most enterprising merchants in the colony. The connection which the father had formed with the Ward family, had a happy effect upon the future destiny of the son. His mother-in-law and her family friends, regardless of expense, bestowed great attention to his early education, which was the best that this country could, at that early period, afford. After completing his primary education, at the best schools at Newport, he was sent to the academy, at Philadelphia, which was reputed to be the best institution, of the kind, in the colonies. It was afterwards the University of Pennsylvania. When he had completed his course of studies there, he entered the office of Judge Trow-bridge, of Cambridge, who was justly esteemed the most profound jurist of his day. Mr. Marchant remained in the office of Judge Trowbridge five years; and was said to be an attentive and severe student. At the termination of his studies, he came to Newport, and commenced practice, under some discouraging circumstances, and others of a more favorable aspect. He was the only dissent-ing, or liberty lawyer, in the colony. His brethren of the high church, then identified with the minis-terial party, viewed him either with contempt, trusting to their power and influence to bear him down; or, with jealousy of his attainments, were indisposed to show him any favor, or to aid his pro-gress. On the other hand, his religious predilec-tions, and his whig principles, obtained for him all the patronage and favor of the friends of freedom. His acquirements, his industry, and forensic talent, soon raised him to the head of his profession. In 1766, Mr. Marchant wrote the deed, from William Read to William Ellery, John Collins, Robert Cooke, and Samuel Fowler, of " Liberty Tree lot," (a large Buttonwood tree standing at the north end of Thames street, Newport,) said lot and tree there-on, were conveyed to the grantees, " in trust, and forever thereafter to be known by the name, of the TREE OF LIBERTY; to be set apart to, and for the use of, the sons of liberty; and that the same

stand as a monument of the spirited and noble opposition made to the STAMP ACT, in the year 1765,
by the sons of liberty, in Newport, and throughout
the continent of North America; and to be considered as emblematical of public liberty; of taking deep root in English America, of her strength
and spreading protection; of her benign influences,
refreshing her sons in all their just struggles,
against the attempts of tyranny and oppression.
And furthermore, the said tree of liberty is destined and set apart, for exposing to public ignominy
and reproach, all offenders against the liberties of
the country, and the abettors and approvers of such
as would enslave her.   And that the same may be
repaired to upon all rejoicings, on account of the
rescue and deliverance of liberty, from any dangers she may have been in, of being subverted or
overthrown.   And furthermore, that the said tree
of liberty stand as a memorial of the firm and unshaken loyalty of the American sons of liberty, to
his Majesty, King George III., and of their inviolable attachment to the happy establishment of the
Protestant succession, in the illustrious House of
Hanover. And in general, said TREE is hereby set
apart, for such other purposes, as they, the true
born sons of liberty shall, from time to time, from
age to age, and in all times and ages hereafter, apprehend, judge and resolve, may subserve the glorious cause of PUBLIC LIBERTY." The deed is wit-

nessed by thirty-one of the most respectable and influential whigs in Newport. When the Island was afterwards possessed by the enemy, this tree, so dedicated, was destroyed; but after the evacuation it was replaced by another which is still standing.

Mr. Marchant was appointed by the legislature to aid in almost all colony prosecutions; and was an efficient member on committees of that body, although not a representative. In early professional life, Mr. Marchant was elected, under the Ward influence, Attorney General of the colony, at the October session, 1770, to fill the vacancy occasioned by the death of Oliver Arnold. Such was the legal ability with which his official duties were discharged, that though opposed, at the next election, by a candidate from the majority party, he was elected, over his opponent, by an overwhelming majority. He continued to sustain the office, through all the vicissitudes of party, until May, 1777.

Being engaged in various appeals to the King in Council, and charged by the colony with the responsibility of aiding Mr. Joseph Sherwood, their resident agent, in London, in the adjustment of claims on the British government; and also to effect a final disposition of the controversy with

8

Massachusetts; and endeavor to procure the appointment of commissioners, by the King in Council, to settle the boundary line between the colonies, Mr. Marchant, in 1771, departed for England. He carried with him, to the mother country, recommendations from gentlemen of the first respectability, in this colony and Massachusetts, to many of the first literary and political characters of Great Britain, particularly of the whig party, to which he had become attached, upon the first division of the country, upon the oppressive exactions of Parliament. With many of the first friends of American liberty, in England and Scotland, he had formed the most intimate acquaintance; which, in some instances, were ripened into friendships, which were continued, by correspondence, for many years after he returned to his native country. Dr. Franklin, whom he had known in Philadelphia, then in London, bestowed on him flattering marks of esteem, and was highly serviceable, in extending his literary and political connexions. He attended the celebrated trial of Summerset, before Lord Mansfield, which deeply impressed the principles of civil liberty on his mind. In a journal he kept during his residence abroad, he minuted his own reflections on this important cause.

In the latter part of the year 1772, he embarked for America. At that period, the difficulties between Great Britain and this country, had assumed a threatening aspect. And though the ministerial party, in the colony, were wealthy and strong in numbers, Mr. Marchant continued true to the principles he had early espoused, and he hesitated not to take an early and decided stand in favor of liberty. He was considered one of the active leaders of the whig party, and one of the most obnoxious individuals to the ministerialists. So much so, that when Walace, with his squadron, lay before Newport, he threatened, if he could catch him, to hang him at the yard-arm. He even searched the boats for this object of his hate and vengeance, who in order to attend the circuits of Washington and Kent counties, was under the necessity of passing round through Providence.

Immediately after the battle of Lexington, Mr. Marchant perceiving that the British would occupy Newport, as an important point, purchased an estate in Narragansett, [where his son, the Hon. William Marchant, now resides,] and removed, with his family, where they remained through the war. During this period, he continued his professional duties, and was engaged in the important causes that arose until the year 1777, when he was elected a delegate to the Continental Congress. He was re-elected in 1778 and 1789. He was one of the signers of the articles of confederation, and while signing, he said, the guns of the battle of Brandywine were roaring in his ears. After that battle,

Congress left Philadelphia, and retired to York-town. During the session of the confederated Congress, Mr. Marchant delivered several speeches, which gained him considerable reputation. He was an efficient member on various important committees, and gained considerable notoriety, in a controversy with the distinguished Judge Chase, of Maryland.

No delegate could be elected to Congress for more than three years, or one term in succession. After the second term, Mr. Marchant was, in 1784, re-elected; but owing to professional engagements, he declined.

The General Assembly, at their May session, passed a vote of thanks to Messrs. William Ellery and Henry Marchant, for the eminent services they had rendered the state in the confederated Congress.

In the spring of 1784, Mr. Marchant returned from his residence in Narragansett, to Newport, and was immediately elected a Representative for that town, to the General Assembly. He continued one of the most active and influential members of that body, until the adoption of the Federal constitution. He was elected a member of the convention for the adoption of that instrument, and made some impressive speeches in its favor.

Upon the organization of the government, under the constitution, he was nominated by Gen. Washiugton, then President of the United States, Judge of the District Court for Rhode-Island, and his nomination was unanimously confirmed. The duties of this office, were discharged with distinguished ability and reputation, until his death. He died August 30th, 1796. His remains were interred in the north burial ground, in Newport, near the Perry monument. A handsome stone is erected to his memory, on which is sculptured a bust, which is said to be a good resemblance of the deceased, with the following inscription:

THE

HON. HENRY MARCHANT,

MEMBER OF THE REVOLUTIONARY CONGRESS, AND UNITED STATES' JUDGE FOR THE DISTRICT OF RHODE-ISLAND.

DIED AUGUST 30, 1796,

ÆTATE 56.

8*

HENRY GOODWIN.

Of Mr. Goodwin, but few incidents have been obtained. When the paper money party triumphed, in the political struggle of 1786, they retained some of their opponents in office. But their influence was actively exerted to defeat the operation of the *paper money tender* laws, the favorite measure of the administration.

The dominant party, in 1787, doubting the policy of keeping their political enemies longer in office, made a " *clean sweep.*" Mr. Goodwin was elected Attorney General, in the place of Mr. Channing, and re-elected the succeeding year. But hesitating to applaud all the measures of the party, and condemning some, they withheld their support.

Mr. Goodwin was a man whose genius was brilliant, but erratic. His eloquence at times, was overpowering; his rhapsodies of expression overflowing. He wrote some fine poetry, and a number of tragedies. It is reported that some of the scenes were admirably wrought, and the descriptions touching and beautiful. Dr. Manning, President of Providence College, now Brown University, observed of him,—"that such a rare genius was not born once in a century."

He was a warm-hearted and high-minded man. The splendor of his eloquence, and the brilliancy of his wit, captivated the public mind; but there was no equality in the ingredients of his character. His error was, that he overdid every thing. He was subject to no restraint. He knew no bounds. His temper was excitable; his passions violent and unmanageable; his invectives so intolerable towards those whom he fancied were obnoxious to him, that he speedily lost public favor. In fact, he unquestionably labored under a partial intellectual derangement. Unfortunately the treatment of this mental disease was but imperfectly understood at that period, even by physicians. After he had been confined to his room, and general admission had been refused, Dr. Senter, the most eminent of the profession, remarked that,—"nothing was the matter with him, only he had *jibed* all standing." Had the "science of mind" been as well understood by the medical faculty then, as now, probably this splendid and eloquent man might have been restored to public usefulness.

Mr. Blake, an attorney at law, in Bristol, at which place Mr. Goodwin married and died, upon diligent enquiry, writes:

" BRISTOL, MARCH 4, 1841.

Dear Sir—I am sorry, that after all this delay,
I can tell you so little of Mr. Goodwin.   But every
fact I can obtain, I give you below. Yours, &c.

JOS. M. BLAKE."

"Henry Goodwin was born in Boston, [it is believed.]   His father was Benjamin Goodwin, who
married Hannah Le Baron, of Plymouth.   Mr.
Henry Goodwin, in 1782, married Mary Bradford,
the daughter of Gov. Bradford, of Bristol.   He
commenced the practice of law in Taunton, and
from thence removed to Newport, where he practi-
ced until his death.   He died at Bristol, while on
a visit at Gov. Bradford's, the 31st of May, 1789."

" He left four children, one son and three daughters.   The son is dead.   The three daughters are
now living."

In addition to which, the Hon. Asher Robbins,
late Senator in Congress, in a communication, dated Newport, March 21, 1841, observes,—

" I was not much acquainted with Mr. Goodwin
personally ; he died before my leaving my place in
Providence college, and coming to Newport to read
law with Mr. Channing; though I had seen him
occasionally at Providence, while he was attending
the General Assembly and courts there; and had

:some slight acquaintance with him; and I had an opportunity to hear him speak on several occasions.

He was very fluent, and his eloquence was very fine; he had a fine voice, and his delivery was very fine; he had brilliant talents, but his learning, I was told, was not profound. He had a great deal of wit, but it was of the keen, sarcastic kind, rather than of the good-natured and pleasant.

In person he was rather above the middle stature, and well proportioned; his countenance rather severe and determined, though with regular, animated features; and according to my recollection, a little pitted with the small pox.

His dress was at the top of the mode, rich and showy. It was an object of particular attention with him. Not one of the bar vied with him in this particular. He was educated, I understood, a t Cambridge.

He was patronised by the paper money party, and they made him Attorney General of the state; but he would not go all lengths with them, and they withdrew their patronage.

In a fit of sickness he became partially deranged; but was convalescent in both body and mind, when the unfortunate accident took place which terminated in his death. He died young, but at what age I do not know."

WILLIAM CHANNING.

It would be deemed an assumption of vanity for another hand to attempt a sketch of the life and character of William Channing, one of the early Attorney Generals of Rhode-Island, while his sons, the Rev. William E. Channing, of Boston, and Dr. E. T. Channing, professor in Harvard University, are living, and so eminently qualified to perform this delicate task. The author has therefore availed himself of the liberal aid of those distinguished gentlemen, in giving to this, otherwise imperfect memoir, an interest far beyond the slight details of the public services of its subject which were within his reach; and he could not yield to the suggestion in the letter of the Rev. Dr. Channing, to suppress any portion of so interesting a tribute of filial affection.

William Channing, in early life, sustained many honorable offices by legislative appointment, and at the annual state election, in 1777, he was, by his fellow citizens, elected Attorney General without opposition; his predecessor, Mr. Marchant, having been, at the same period, chosen delegate to the confederated Congress. He was annually re-elected to the same office, until 1787, when with the Governor, Senate, and House of Representatives, he was swept away by the paper money tornado of 1785, the emission of which, by the dominant party in the legislature, he conscientiously and unflinchingly opposed. When the ebullitions of the political caldron had subsided, and the public mind had returned to its sober judgment, the freemen doubly honored him by re-electing him in 1791, to the same honorable station, from which he had been ejected by the paper money party, in addition to the office of District Attorney of the United States for the district of Rhode-Island, both of which he conjunctively held until his death.

The sovereign position the state had assumed after the Declaration of Independence, and the variety of laws enacted, growing out of the revolution, embracing the confiscation and maratime acts, imposed on the Attorney General, new, arduous and responsible duties, which by the concurrent testimony of the Hon. Judge Bourne, the Hon. Elisha R. Potter, and the Hon. William Hunter, were by Mr. Channing discharged with eminent ability, energy and devotion.

The letter of Dr. Channing, in answer to one soliciting his aid in this contemplated memoir, with the enclosure from his brother, and the obituary by the late Hon. William Ellery, are as follows:

" CAMBRIDGE, NOV. 12, 1840.

I give you all I know relating to the subject of Mr. Updike's letter. William Channing was the second son of John Channing, of Newport, Rhode-Island, merchant.

He was grandson of John Channing, of Dorsetshire, England; the first of the name who came to America, and who arrived in Boston about 1715. He was born in Newport, May 31, 1751, and was educated at Nashua Hall, (Princeton College,) where he graduated in 1769.

In May, 1773, he was married to Lucy Ellery, daughter of William Ellery, of Newport, [one of the signers of the Declaration of Independence,] by whom he had eleven children, nine of whom were living at his death.

He died at Newport, Sept. 21, 1793, after an illness of three months. Grandfather Ellery wrote a character of him immediately after his death, which was intended for the papers, but never published. He gave me the manuscript. The sketch is striking, and perhaps would be useful for Mr. Updike's purposes. If, on seeing it, you should think so, I will copy it for him.

I have heard testimonies from many, to the great sweetness of his spirit, and of his entire trust-worthiness in his many and important vocations.

I remember as long ago as 1813 hearing, from Judge Dawes, an account of his appearance in court. The Judge met him frequently at Taunton. He described his style of speaking as remarkable for its sweet fluency. He called it 'mellifluous.' ·

I know how difficult it is at this time of day to present any image of such a character to the public, which will give an adequate idea of him. Still I hope you may be able to do something; and certainly the attempt is so modest which Mr. Updike is making, that even a little, if but true, will be no injustice to the memory of our father, and may be of service to others.   Yours truly,

E. T. CHANNING.

To Dr. W. E. Channing."

"Boston. Dec. 18, 1841.

My Dear Sir,—I received, with great pleasure, your letter of last month, in which you inform me that you are preparing " the biography of the Rhode-Island Bar," and request me to furnish any materials in my power for a memoir of my father. My recollections of my father are imperfect, as he died when I was thirteen years of age, and I had been sent from home before that event. But the many testimonies which I have received to his eminence as a lawyer, as well as to his private virtues, make me desirous that there should be some me-

9

morial of him.   My brother, Professor E. T. Channing, who is the antiquary of the family, has sent
me, in a letter, which I enclose, such facts as he has
been able to gather; and has also furnished me
with a sketch of my father's character, prepared
by my venerable grandfather, William Ellery.
This, as you will see, is a tribute of affection; but
my grandfather was remarkable for his honesty,
which almost amounted to bluntness; and I am
confident that his language, however strong, did
not go beyond his convictions.   I cheerfully add
my own reminiscences, and a few facts.

" My father retained much attachment to Princeton college, where he was educated, so that he
thought of sending me there.   He was the class-
mate and friend of Samuel S. Smith, afterwards
distinguished as a theologian, and as the President
of that institution.   In the last part of his collegiate days he enjoyed the instructions of the celebrated Dr. Witherspoon.

"His early marriage, and the rapid increase of
his family, obliged him to confine himself rigidly
to his profession.   He was too busy to give much
time to general reading, or even to his family.
Still I have distinct impressions of his excellence
in his social relations.   He was the delight of the
circle in which he moved.   His mother, brothers
and sisters leaned on him as on no other.   I well

remember the benignity of his countenance and voice. At the same time he was a strict disciplinarian at home, and according to the mistaken notions of that time, kept me at too great a distance from him. In truth, the prevalent notions of education were much more imperfect than in our day.

"I often went into courts, but was too young to understand my father's merits in the profession; but I had always heard of him as standing at its head. My brother says, that Judge Dawes used to speak of his style and manner as 'mellifluous,' but at times he was vehement; for I well recollect, that I left the court house in fear, at hearing him indignantly reply to, what seemed to him, unworthy language in the opposite counsel.

" His parents were religious, and the impressions made on his young mind were never lost. He was the main pillar of the religious society to which he belonged. The house of worship had suffered much from the occupation of Newport by the British army, so as to be unfit for use; and I recollect few things in my childhood more distinctly than his zeal in restoring it to its destination, and in settling a minister. I cannot doubt that his religious character received important aid from the ministry and friendship of Dr. Styles, who was as eminent for piety as learning, and under whose teachings he grew up. He had a deep, I may say peculiar,

abhorrence of the vice of profaneness; and such
was his influence, that his large family of sons escaped this taint to a remarkable degree, though
brought up in the midst of it. I recollect, with
gratitude, the strong impression which he made on
my own mind. I owed it to him that, though living in the atmosphere of this vice, no profane word
ever passed my lips.

" On one subject I think of his state of mind with
sorrow. His father, like most respectable merchants of that place, possessed slaves imported
from Africa. They were the domestics of the family; and my father had no sensibility to the evil.
I remember, however, with pleasure, the affectionate relation which subsisted between him and the
Africans, [most of them aged,] who continued to
live with my grandfather. These were liberated
after the revolution; but nothing could remove
them from their old home, where they rather ruled
than served. One of the females used to speak of
herself as the daughter of an African prince; and
she certainly had much of the bearing of royalty.
The dignity of her aspect and manner bespoke an
uncommon woman. She was called Duchess, probably on account of the rank she had held in her
own country. I knew her only after she was free,
and had an establishment of her own. Now and then
she invited all the children of the various families,
to which she was connected, to a party; and we

were liberally feasted under her hospitable roof. My father won the hearts of all his domestics. One of the sincerest mourners at his death, was an excellent woman, who had long lived with us, and whom he honored for her piety.

" I recollect, distinctly, the great interest he took in the political questions which agitated the country. Though but eight or nine years of age, I was present when the Rhode-Island convention adopted the Federal constitution; and the enthusiasm of that moment, I can never forget. My father entered with his whole heart into that unbounded exultation. He was one of the most devoted members of the Federal party. At the beginning of the French revolution, he shared in the universal hope and joy which it inspired; but I well recollect the sadness with which he talked to us one Sunday afternoon of the execution of Louis XVI.; and from that moment his hopes died.

" You speak of the testimony borne to him, by the late Elisha R. Potter, Esq. My father was among the first to discover the abilities of that remarkable man ; and I remember the kindness with which he used to receive him. His spirit was, in truth, the kindest. He was ever ready to see and appreciate superior talents, and to attach himself to worth. His friendship seemed to me, singularly

9*

strong for a man so immersed in business. Among
his friends, were George Champlin, Esq., a politi-
cian of singular sagacity, and who was said to have
ruled the state for years, without forfeiting his integrity; Dr. Isaac Senter, a physician of extensive practice, who was thought to unite, with great
experience, a rare genius in his profession, and
whose commanding figure rises before me, at the
distance of forty-five years, as a specimen of manly
beauty, worthy the chisel of a Grecian sculptor;
and the Rev. Dr. Hitchcock, of Providence, a man
of great sweetness of temper, and who deserves the
grateful remembrance of that city for his zealous
efforts in the cause of public education. My father
took a great pleasure in the society of ministers;
and always welcomed them to his hospitable dwelling.

" I remember his tastes with pleasure. He had
two gardens, one of them quite large, and as he
sought to have every thing which he cultivated of
the best kind, our table, otherwise simple, was, in
this respect, luxurious. He was not satisfied with
what contented his neighbors, but introduced new
varieties of vegetables into the town. He also took
great interest in sacred music. On Sunday even-
ings the choir of the congregation, which included
most of the younger members, and other amateurs,
met in his office for practice in singing. The apart-
ment, somewhat spacious, was filled; and the ani-

mation of the meeting, to which his zeal contributed not a little, made the occasion one of my
weekly pleasures.

"As far as I can trust my recollections of my
father's person, it must have been very prepossessing; but to me, his appearance, at the time, was
more venerable than beautiful. His head was bald;
and his cocked hat, and the other parts of his dress,
which according to the fashions of the day, differed
much from the costume of the young, made him
seem from the first, an old man.

"He prospered in life, but without being able to
leave a competence for his large family. His labors were great, but I have no recollection of seeing him depressed. I should place him among the
happy. He was taken away in the midst of usefulness and hope. The disease of which he died, was
not understood. I remember that he used to com-
plain of feelings which we now should consider as
dyspepsy; but that disease was little thought of
then, and the name never heard.

"These are very scanty reminiscences; but as I
hardly saw my father after reaching my twelfth
year, and as nearly fifty years have passed since
that time, it is not to be wondered at that I can recall no more of his calm, uniform life. The career
of a professional man, occupied with the support

of a large family, offers no great events. But you may select a few hints from what I have now written, and I beg you to suppress every thing which may seem to you unimportant. I little thought, when I began, of writing so much; but the pleasure which all men take in the virtues of parents, has led me on insensibly.

"My father died before I could requite him for his toils for my support, and his interest in my moral well-being; and I feel as if, in this present instance, I was discharging some part, though a very small one, of my great debt. I owed him much, and it is not my smallest obligation that his character enables me to join affectionate esteem and reverence with my instinctive gratitude.

Very truly, yours,
W. E. CHANNING."

Subsequent to the communication of the Rev. Dr. Channing, the Hon. Asher Robbins, late a member of the Senate of the United States, in a letter dated Newport, March 21, 1841, furnished the following facts within his recollection.

"William Channing, Esq., was educated at Princeton, New Jersey, and was cotemporary with Judge Patterson, one of the associate Justices of the U. S. Supreme Court; he read law with Oliver Arnold, at Providence—a self-made man, but a good lawyer. Mr. Arnold was Attorney General of the state; and according to my information, died, while in that office, at Kingston, having gone there to attend a court.

" Mr. Channing was very well read in the law, especially in the forms of pleading; law cases were his favorite reading, even for amusement. He had a large library, and one very well selected.

"He interested himself much in state politics, and his office was the central point of rendezvous, where the leading men congregated for their consultations.

" He was very popular in the state; was Attorney General and District Attorney at the same time; and held both offices at the time of his death.

"His manner of speaking at the bar, was rapid, vehement, and impressive; never studied, nor exactly methodical in his pleadings; but he always came well prepared as to matter and authority. He had an extensive practice, attended all the courts of the state regularly, and was considered, for several years before his death, as the leading counsel of the state. He died, I think, at about forty; and after a short illness.

" In person he was of the middle stature, well made, erect, and of an open countenance; he was lively and pleasant in his conversation, and much disposed to social intercourse; he was hospitable, and kind-hearted. His agreeable manners was one great source of his general popularity.

" In dress he was not remarkable for any particular; his was always proper and becoming, though not an object of much attention with him; the color was commonly black; indeed I do not recollect ever to have seen him in any other.

"His temper was remarkably good, as was his manners; mild, liberal, generous; his habits were all correct; temperate, industrious, mindful, and observant of all the duties and proprieties of life."

The following sketch of the character of William Channing was written by his father-in-law, William Ellery, during the week of Mr. Channing's death. It is copied from the manuscript.

OBITUARY.

WILLIAM CHANNING, ESQ., OF NEWPORT.

Early in life he entered upon the stage of action, and performed his part with such diligence, propriety, and integrity, as procured him not only the affection of his fellow citizens, and the esteem of the state at large, but the notice of the President of the United States.

The law was his profession, and by the study and practice of it, he rose to distinguished eminence.

In the year 1771, he began the practice of the law, and in 1778 [1777] he was appointed Attorney General of the state, and upon the adoption of the Federal constitution, without any solicitation on his part, he was appointed to the office of District Attorney for the district of Rhode-Island, and continued in the faithful and skilful discharge of the duties of these offices, and in the unremitted pursuit of his profession as long as his health would permit, which suffered but little interruption until his last sickness, which confined him to his house about three months, and in the forty-third year of his age put an end to his usefulness.

He repeatedly served as a Deputy for his native town, and such was his regard for its interests, that he did not decline that service until by the extensiveness of his practice, and the increase of his family, he was compelled to give to them his whole attention.

He early became the head of a family. He married in the twenty-third year of his age, and performed the offices and charties of a husband and father, with strict, constant, and tender attention, and was beloved and respected.

The law of kindness and benevolence was in his heart, and on his tongue. The persons employed by him as domestics, and in other services, he treated with great humanity, and rewarded with a liberal punctuality. He was an obedient and respectful son, and a most affectionate brother and friend. To the poor he was compassionate. The needy never went away from his house empty. His table and his purse were always open to their wants, and his munificence was ever accompanied with a sweetness in the manner, which doubled the obligations of gratitude.

His religious sentiments were liberal. He was particularly attached to the Congregational denomination of christians, but he treated all good men of all denominations with kindness and respect. He generously contributed to the support of christian worship in the society to which he belonged, and countenanced and encouraged it by a constant and reverential attendance, and the ministers of religion experienced his hospitality.

His political sentiments were displayed in a warm attachment to the rights of mankind, chastened by a love of peace and order; and his ardent wish was that that species of government might take place in the several societies of men, which would be productive of the greatest happiness.

His countenance and deportment expressed the amiableness and benevolence of his disposition ; and 'his morals corresponded with his manners. He was temperate and honest; he was courteous and respectful. As he keenly felt the distresses of mankind, so he was as strongly disposed to relieve their sufferings. He looked down with such pity on the poor and af-

cour, and like a brother, he wiped away their tears.

Such was the character whose influence and usefulness are for the wisest and most gracious purposes withdrawn from us; but while the widow and fatherless children, all his relations and connections, this town, and this state, and all who knew him, express the deepest regret at their loss, this consolation remains to soothe their grief, that " their loss is his gain."

The following obituary notice is extracted from the Newport Mercury, of September 20, 1793.

Died, at Newport, (Sept. 17, 1793,) in the forty-second year of his age, William Channing, Esq., Attorney General of this State, and Attorney for the U. States for the District of Rhode-Island, an eminent practitioner of the law. An eulogium upon his merits, in private life, would be interesting only to those who are already too deeply wounded at his loss. The approving and unanimous voice of his fellow-citizens, in the various and important offices he has sustained, has rendered his character too conspicuous to be diminished by envy or heightened by praise.

ROUSE J. HELME,

DESCENDED from a family of great respectability and influence in this state. Mr. James Helme, his father, sustained the honorable appointments of Judge of the Common Pleas, and of the Supreme court previous to the revolution, the duties of which were discharged with reputation. Rouse J. Helme was respectably educated under the instructions of a private tutor, as but few at that period could obtain a liberal education. The agitations of the colonial controversy necessarily attracted public attention to other and more vital subjects;— and during the convulsion, our colleges and our churches were, from necessity, converted into barracks, to shelter the war-wearied soldier, or hospitals for the reception of the sick and wounded. Well instructed foreigners, who were unable to return to the mother country, or chose to remain under our institutions, were the principal instructors in the higher branches of education, and such were principally engaged by the families of the opulent. Mr. Helme was well instructed in mathematics, surveying, geography, astronomy, and in latin—rather an advanced education for that period—by a preceptor of the description mentioned.

Predilection for the study of the law early displayed itself, and to promote his views, his father placed him under the instruction of Matthew Robinson, Esq., who was justly estimated one of the most learned lawyers and able special pleaders of the times; to which may be added, that he possessed one of the best selected libraries extant. He continued in the office of Mr. Robinson three years, and commenced practice in South Kingstown, his native town. He soon acquired, by his attentive habits and courteous manners, a large share of business. He early embarked in colonial politics, and becoming a favorite of his party, was soon elevated to offices of trust and confidence, and held various appointments indicative of activity and talent.

In Oct. 1776,   He was elected Deputy Secretary to the General Assembly, and was successively re-elected until May, 1778.

Feb'y. 1777,   He was elected clerk of the council of war, which office he held until the passage of the act re-organizing that body in May, 1778.

Sept. 1777,   He was elected one of the committee with Gov. Bradford, Henry Ward, William Channing, and Jonathan Arnold, to form a plan of government, and lay the same before the legislature.

Oct. 1777,   He was appointed clerk of the committee, raised by the General Assembly, to enquire into the reasons of the failure of Gen. Spencer's expedition.

Dec. 1777,   He was appointed one of the committee to draught a bill for confiscating and selling the estates of disaffected persons.

Feb'y 1778,   He was one of the committee to prepare a bill prescribing and establishing an oath of fidelity and allegiance to the state.

May, 1778,   He was elected a representative to the General Assembly, to which office he was successively re-elected for eight years.

He was appointed, with Theodore Foster, a committee to draught a bill, in pursuance to the resolve of Congress, for granting pardons.

Also elected a member of the council of war for Kings county.

May, 1771,   He was appointed by the General Assembly to assist the Attorney General in the trial of certain offenders in the county of Kent, charged with supplying the enemy.

Oct. 1779,   Gen. Varnum and Mr. Helme were appointed a committee to draught a bill, laying an embargo upon all goods whatever in this state.

July, 1780,   John I. Clark, William Channing, R. J. Helme, M. Bowler and Benjamin Bourne, Esq'rs, were appointed, by the General Assembly, a committee to draught addresses, in behalf of the legislature, to the officers of the French fleet, who reported the following, to the Hon. Gen. le Compte de Rochambeau, and Le Chevalier de Ternay:

"The representatives of the state of Rhode-Island and Providence Plantations, in General Assembly convened, with the most pleasing satisfaction, take the earliest opportunity of congratulating Compte de Rochambeau, Lieutenant General of the army of his most Christian Majesty, upon his safe arrival

10*

within the United States.　Upon this occasion we cannot be too expressive of the grateful sense we entertain for the generous and magnanimous aid afforded to the United States by their illustrious friend and ally.　Sufficient has been the proofs of his zeal and friendship.　The present instance must constrain even envious disappointed Britons, to venerate the wisdom of his councils, and the sincerity of his noble mind. We look forward with the most pleasing expectation to the end of a campaign in which the allied force of France and these United States, under the smiles of Providence, may be productive of peace and happiness to the contending powers and mankind in general.　We assure you, sir, our expectations are enlarged, when we consider the wisdom of his most christian majesty in your appointment, as the commander of his army destined to our assistance.　Be assured, sir, of every exertion in the power of this state to afford the necessary refreshments to the army under your command, and to render the service to all ranks as agreeable and happy, as it is honorable.

We are, in behalf of the General Assembly, the General's most obedient, and most devoted humble servants.

Lieut. Gen. Compte de Rochambeau."

"The representatives of the state of Rhode-Island and Providence Plantations, in General Assembly convened, with the most pleasing satisfaction, take

this, the earliest opportunity, of testifying the sentiments, that are impressed upon them by the great
attention which his most christian majesty has invariably manifested to the United States. The
formidable armament heretofore sent to our aid,
have essentially promoted our happiness and independence; but at a time when Europe is involved
in the calamities of war, by the ambitious views of
the British court, we cannot express the gratitude
we feel upon your arrival, with the fleet under your
command, destined bv our illustrious friend and
ally'to the assistance of the United States. We
entreat you, on this occasion, to accept the warmest congratulations of the General Assembly of the
state of Rhode-Island and Providence Plantations.
And be assured, sir, of every exertion in their
power to afford the necessary refreshments to the
fleet, and to render the service as agreeable and
happy as it is honorable

We are, in behalf of the General Assembly, the
Admiral's most obedient and most humble servants.

Le Chevelier de Ternay."

Jan. 1781.   Mr. Helme was elected clerk of the
             Assembly, and re-elected in May,
             1781.

June, 1782. Gen. Varnum and Mr. Helme were
             appointed a committee, to pre-
             pare a bill, pursuant to a resolve

of Congress, relative to the in-
fractions of the LAW OF NATIONS
—also, an act prescribing a more
speedy method of administering
justice between citizens of the
United States and France, our
ally. Also, concerning shipwreck-
ed property.

Dec. 1783.   Archibald Crary, R. J. Helme and
Gen. Varnum, were appointed a
committee to draught an address
in the name of the legislature, to
the Hon. Major General Nathaniel Greene, on his return to this
state; which was reported as follows :

"Sir,—The Governor and company, in General
Assembly convened, present to you their sincerest
congratulations, upon your happy return to this
state.   When they appointed you to the most honorable office in the service of your country, they
anticipated the great events which have more than
justified their expectations.

Your military conduct and achievements, so
brilliant through the whole revolution, have excited an unabated affection in the breasts of those
who are friendly to the rights of mankind.   The

citizens of this state, in particular, will hold you dear, while the tribute of praise is rendered only to the claims of virtue. May the same divine beneficence which has secured to this state the blessings of peace and independence, continue to you every felicity that worthy actions estimated by gratitude and affection deserve.

Your obedient and humble servants."

GENERAL GREENE'S ANSWER.

"*To the Governor and company in General Assembly.*

My bosom is warm with gratitude from your kind and affectionate address. As it has ever been my pride to deserve your good opinion, so it is my highest pride to meet your approbation. I feel myself wedded to the interest and happiness of this state from my earliest attachments. It gives me the most pleasing satisfaction to promote its interest and welfare.

Permit me to return my most respectful acknowledgments for the honor you have done me, and for the interest you take in my present and future happiness.

I have the honor to be, gentlemen, with all possible respect, your most obedient servant,

NATHANIEL GREENE."

May, 1784. **Mr.** Helme was appointed one of the committee to take into considera-

tion the petition of the artificers
of Newport.

June, 1785,   He was appointed one of the committee, with Gen. Varnum and
Oliver Davis, to meet a committee appointed by the legislature
of Connecticut, to regulate the
fisheries in Pawcatuck river.

Oct. 1785,   He was appointed on the committee
to draught an act for manning
Fort Washington.

Feb. 1786,   He was appointed a committee, with
Col. Jeremiah Olney, to report
monthly, the allowances to the
invalid soldiers.

The paper money party, in May, 1786, elected
Gov. Collins over Gov. Greene. In this election
no less than thirty-eight representatives were removed; among the number, was Mr. Helme. The
paper money party, though conscientiously opposed
on principles of rectitude, now triumphed, and
consequences the most disastrous to public faith
and morals, upon the reckless emission of irredeemable paper, by the legislature, ensued.

On the trial of the Judges of the Supreme Court before the General Assembly, at their October session, 1786, for adjudging in the case of Trevett vs. Weeden, the paper money tender laws, " unconstitutional and void," a motion was made by a member, and agreed to, " that the opinion of the Attorney General, [William Channing, Esq.,] be taken, and the sentiments of other professional gentlemen requested, whether constitutionally and agreeable to law, the General Assembly can suspend or remove from office the Judges of the Supreme Court, without a previous charge and statement of criminality, due process, trial and conviction thereon."

After the Attorney General and the Hon. Mr. Bradford had addressed the House, Mr. Helme rose and made the following pertinent and sound remarks.   He said, "the subject was new to him, and he was not fully prepared to give an opinion. But, at present, he was inclined to think, that there was no constitutional law by which the question could be solved;—that therefore it must be in the breast of the General Assembly to point out the mode of trial, by an act for that purpose, should a trial be thought necessary.   If they proceed to try the Judges, either by themselves, or a court to be appointed specially for that purpose, they must cause them first to be impeached, and state the facts particularly upon which the impeachment is

founded; the common law will direct in the manner of process, and should they be found guilty,
they cannot be removed from their offices but by
bill in the nature of a bill of ATTAINDER, which
must pass both Houses and be enacted into a law."

Mr. Helme being an able lawyer, and a skilful
draughtman, his services were found to be so highly requisite in conducting the business of the legislature, that the dominant party, though politically
opposed to him, at the May session, 1787, elected
him clerk of the House of Representatives, and
testified their approbation of his ability by repeated re-elections.

Being unable to break through the strength of
the paper money influence in South Kingstown,
Mr. Helme, in May, 1788, was returned a representative to the legislature from New Shoreham, under the act, passed during the revolution, permit-
ting that town, (being an island) to elect members
from the main.

In May, 1789, he was again returned a member
from New Shoreham, and continued their representative until his death, on the 13th of October following. His remains were interred in the Presbyterian burial ground, on Tower hill, in South Kings-

town, where his ancestors repose. Suitable grave-stones were erected to his memory, with the following inscription :

IN MEMORY OF

ROUSE J. HELME

WHO DEPARTED THIS LIFE OCT. 13, 1789, IN THE 46th YEAR
OF HIS AGE.

" And the servant said, Lord it is done as thou has commanded, and yet there is room.

11

JOHN COLE

Was the son of Elisha Cole, of North Kingstown, in the county of Kings, now Washington, in this state, who was for many years a member of the state Senate, and estimated as one of the largest landholders in the county. John obtained an early, reputable education in the English branches; and was well instructed under a foreign instructor in the Latin and Greek languages. He studied law in the office of Daniel Updike, Esq., then Attorney General of the Colony, married his daughter Mary, and commenced practice in Providence, under his patronage. Mr. Cole's attention to business soon obtained for him a good share of practice in the county, and a considerable on the circuits.

In 1763, he was elected an associate Justice of the Supreme court of the colony; and at the January session of the General Assembly, 1764, he was promoted to the chair of Chief Justice, in the place of John Bannister, who resigned. At the succeeding annual election in May, he was re-elected to the same honorable office. At this period the agitations in the colonies, respecting the stamp act, arose. Lord Grenville, the prime minister, in the winter of 1764, announced to the agents of the colonies, his intention of drawing a revenue from America. The existing sugar act was enforced by new provisions, at the session of the parliament in April, and the Stamp act, although introduced, was postponed to the next session. All breaches of the first mentioned act, were to be prosecuted in the Vice Admiralty courts, independent of colonial legislation. To further the tyrannical project, naval commanders were constituted revenue officers, and the colonists were greatly harrassed and distressed by seizures under them. These ministerial and parliamentary measures were promptly communicated to the colonies by their respective agents in England. The states at once took the alarm, particularly at the contemplated Stamp act. The people of Boston, at their town meeting, in May, 1764, instructed their representatives at the General Court, in the most decisive manner; and at their ensuing October session, the General Court remonstrated in a firm and expressive tone against the exactions of the home

The people of the colonies were not only addressed by their respective legislatures, and through the press, but in spirited pamphlets, by the ablest hands. Those by Otis and Thatcher were particularly distinguished. Among the patriotic cham-

pions of American liberty, at this excited crisis,
appeared Gov. Hopkins, in a pamphlet, entitled—
" The rights of the colonies examined." It was
presented to the legislature in manuscript. At
their November session, 1764, the General Assembly requested the author to finish and transmit it
to our agent in London, for publication and distri-
bution. This work is represented to have been
executed with great ability and talent, and it is to
be regretted that a copy cannot now be found.

The people of Rhode-Island, as resolute as any
of her sister colonies in resistance to the unconstitutional requisitions of the British government, felt
a lively indignation, that their previous remonstrances had proved unavailing. Conscious that their
rights had been insultingly neglected, the General
Assembly, in July, of the same year, appointed a
committee to confer with the committees of the
other colonies, respecting the sugar act, and to remonstrate against the intended Stamp act. The
legislature of Massachusetts having issued a spirited address, the legislature of this state, at their
October session, in 1764, appointed Mr. Cole a
committee to repair to Boston, and obtain a copy
for their use, and adjourned to November. At the
last mentioned session, the General Assembly passed strong and energetic resolutions, in unison with
the other colonies, which were transmitted to our

agent in London; and appointed a committee, of which Mr. Cole was one, to act and correspond during the recess, with the committees of the legislatures of the other colonies, and to remonstrate against the present burthens, and especially against the Stamp act. Judge Cole was an active and influential member of the various committees. But the home government, regardless of colonial remonstrances, and deaf to the entreaties of our agent, passed the Stamp act " bill in the House of Commons, by a vote of 250 to 50. It was adopted in the House of Lords with great unanimity, and on the 22d of March received the royal sanction."

This flagrant act of oppression created a violent excitement in the colonies. Massachusetts appointed commissioners to meet such commissioners as should be appointed by the other colonies, at New-York, in October, 1765, to consult together, and address the King and Parliament for relief.

Mr. Cole's strong whig principles, popularity and uncompromising opposition to the taxation of the colonies, brought him into the legislature, [having resigned the office of Chief Justice,] as a representative from Providence.

" The people of Rhode-Island were among the
11*

first to appoint commissioners to meet at New-
York, and the most determined in their opposition
to the acts imposing taxes upon them. The inhabitants of Providence, on the seventh of August, in
town meeting, resolved, 'to give instructions to
their representatives in General Assembly, concerning the Stamp act, and other matters;' and appointed Stephen Hopkins, John Cole, Nicholas
Cooke, Samuel Nightingale, James Angell, John
Brown, and Silas Downer, a committee to draw up
such instructions. The committee reported, that
their representatives be instructed to procure the
adoption of the whole of the resolutions which
had been published, as the acts of the Virginia assembly, with the exception of the last. The report was unanimously adopted by the inhabitants
of the town. They not only declared that the'
Stamp act was 'unconstitutional, and had a manifest tendency to destroy British as well as American liberty,' but that his Majesty's liege people,
the inhabitants of the colony, were not bound to
yield to any law or ordinance, designed to impose
any internal taxation whatever upon them, other
than the laws and ordinances of this General Assembly."

"They also instructed their representatives to
procure an act to be passed, declaring that the
courts of common law alone, and not courts of Ad-

miralty, have, and ought to have jurisdiction in all cases growing or arising in this colony, on account of levying or collecting any internal taxes, or of any matter relating thereto; and that such process, or way of trial, shall hereafter be had and used in such matters as have been usual and accustomed, time out of mind; and further, that no decree of any court of Admiralty respecting these matters, shall be executed in this colony."

The General Assembly adopted the resolutions recommended by the citizens of Providence, with an additional one more energetic and unwavering in determination than any other colony at this early period of resistance. The General Assembly directed, *" all officers to proceed in the execution of their respective offices, in the same manner as usual, and that the Assembly would indemnify and save harmless all said officers on account of their conduct agreeable to this resolution."*

Judge Cole was elected a representative from Providence through the stormy period of 1766, and at the May session, 1767, was promoted to the chair of Speaker of the House, and in August declined a re-election.

In 1770, and for several years preceding, great complaints had existed against the gross inequality and injustice of the general estimate of taxation, and its disproportionate operation upon the respective towns. South Kingstown warmly protested against its oppression. In a state tax of £12000, South Kingstown was assessed £1009, Providence, £766, and others in a similar ratio. This injustice was so apparent, and the complaints so loud, that the legislature, in May, appointed Mr. Cole and others, a committee to enquire into their grievances, but no relief was granted or remedy proposed. The representatives from the towns which had increased in corporate wealth, since the previous estimate, governed by the interests of their constituents, uniting with those who did not anticipate any

---

Col. Edward Cole was the brother of John. He was Colonel of a regiment under Gen. Wolf, at the seige of Quebec, in 1759. He also commanded a regiment at the capture of Havana, under the Earl of Albemarle. He was afterwards commissioned by Sir William Johnson, superintendent of Indian affairs, under the Crown, to treat with the Indians in the west, and was conducted by Indian guides through the forests of the now State of Ohio. On this mission he encountered great perils, and endured severe sufferings. Upon his return, he settled at Newport. At the commencement of the Revolution, in opposition to his brother, he adhered to the cause of the Crown. He was insulted—his house entered—and his furniture and pictures much mutilated. He fled to the British; was a Colonel in the King's service; and after the war he settled in Nova Scotia, and was allowed a pension of £150 per annum, during life; he died at an advanced age.

benefit from the change, continued to refuse re-
dress. This irritating inequality and manifest oppression, continued to exist until the appearance
in the legislature of the Hon. Elisha R. Potter, in
the year 1793. Through his talents and influence
the estimate of 1795, was effected. This Hercu-
lean triumph, against the efforts of the Providence
delegation, secured to Mr. Potter the zealous support of the minority towns, and South Kingstown in
particular, through life.

In February, 1775, the General Assembly constituted a Maritime or Vice-Admiralty court for
this state. John Foster was appointed Judge, and
Mr. Cole, Advocate General, which office he sustained during his life.

Mr. Cole, for many years, sustained the office of
President of the town council of the town of Providence, by successive elections, and discharged the
duties with reputation.

Professionally, it is enough to state, that General
Varnum uniformly spoke of Mr. Cole as an advocate of respectable talents. He was a handsome
speaker, reputed a sound Lawyer and sustained a
fair and honorable character. He was large in
person, six feet in height, corpulent, and severely
afflicted with the gout. In advanced life he was

induced to enter a small pox hospital for inocula-
tion, to avoid the infection which was prevalent
during the revolution. Being gross, aged, and his
constitution being otherwise impaired, the disease
proved fatal, and he died in the hospital, October,
1777, and was buried in the hospital grounds.

ARCHIBALD CAMPBELL

" A COLONY of Scotch emigrants, embracing the Campbells, Stewarts, Kennedys, Wylies, and Hunters, with others, settled in Voluntown, in Conneccut, about one hundred and fifty years ago. The object of leaving their native land, was the better enjoyment of religious liberty. They were generally well informed, and pious ;—they soon establish a church upon the congregational plan; it is still in a flourishing condition. They possessed considerable property; were industrious and friendly. Hundreds of their posterity have emigrated to New York and Ohio and are noted for being friendly to religion and education."*

The subject of this memoir migrated from Voluntown, and settled at East Greenwich, in Rhode-Island, about the year 1750, and commenced the practice of the law in Kent county, but with what reputation cannot now be ascertained. Whether Mr. Campbell was liberally educated, or regularly studied the profession, is not known. He continued

---

* Extract from a letter of D. Campbell, of Voluntown.

in his profession, at East Greenwich, until his
death, and obtained a large share of practice in the
county, and considerable on the circuits. From the
distinction of his ancestry, it would be conjectured
that he was learned in the general sciences, and
well instructed in the law; and we are induced to
believe, from general reputation, that his professional acquirements were highly respectable. He
was popular, and greatly esteemed by the public
generally, for probity of character. The town of
East Greenwich, in 1768, elected him their representative to the General Assembly of the colony.
Mr. Campbell was an efficient member of the legislature, and was appointed on various important
committees; one to draw up an act of Bankruptcy
for the colony, and was chairman of the committee
of which Mr. George Jackson, and the Attorney
General, Oliver Arnold, were associates, to draught
an act to limit and restrain the issuing of *Writs of
Error* to carry cases to England for trial—a imn-
portant movement of the colonial legislature, to
arrest the supervising power of the mother country—showing that the body politic followed the
impulse of the people, in steadily marching up to
the great epoch of '76· Mr. Campbell's being
placed at the head of this committee, is a sufficient
guaranty that he was an unwavering supporter of
colonial liberty; and one, in whose integrity, its
friends could confide. He was re-elected to the

same honorable office as long as his health would permit. His constituents were shortly deprived of the benefits of his talents and usefulness; he died in the succeeding year. " Mr. Campbell was a gentleman of handsome address, reputed an excellent man, a good counsellor, plain speaker, but not an eloquent advocate." His stature was of the common height, and in person slender. He left one son, named Jacob, and three daughters

In the Baptist burial ground, in East Greenwich, a handsome grave stone is erected to his memory. More information is transmitted to us respecting him, from the following inscription upon it, than from any other source now extant.

IN MEMORY OF
ARCHIBALD CAMPBELL, Esquire,
SON OF ARCHIBALD, AND GRANDSON OF THE REV'D DANIEL CAMPBELL, AND NEPHEW OF THE REV'D JOHN CAMPBELL,
LATE PRESIDENT OF THE
COLLEGE OF GLASCOW,
WHO DEPARTED THIS LIFE, OCT. 16, 1769.
IN THE
41st YEAR OF HIS AGE.

Viator ecce patria columen
Juris pressicum benignum genitorem
Et indulgentissmus maritum.
Englished thus:
Traveller, behold the patriot, the lawyer,
The kind father, and the most indulgent husband.

JACOB CAMPBELL,

Was the only son of Archibald Campbell, Esq., —was born in East Greenwich, in 1760, and graduated from Rhode-Island College in September, 1783, with the reputation of a fine scholar. After he left college he was preceptor of a classical school in East Greenwich for a short time, and then entered the office of Gen. Varnum as a student at law. Daniel Updike, William Greene, Ray Greene, John Bowman, and George Tillinghast, were students in the same office. Campbell was admitted to the bar, and opened an office in East Greenwich, and did some business in his profession. His talents and acquirements entitled him to a full share of practice, but Gen. Varnum residing in the same place, much could not have been anticipated, for he overshadowed all. During his leisure hours he devoted his mind to classic literature and poetry.

The natural temperament of Campbell was unfortunate. His disposition was jaundiced—he was proud spirited, and occasionally dejected—was early and deeply imbued with jealousy. With a mind sensitive and nervous, he was borne down with fancied suspicions of intended injury and neglect. The ostentatious manner of Mr. Ray Greene filled him with an unbearable antipathy. If Mr. Greene entered the social circle where he was, any asylum would be peace to his sensitive genius.

The legislature, after the peace of 1783, ordered the sheriffs to read the definitive treaty of peace, and the proclamation of Congress, announcing its consummation, at the Court houses of their respective counties. Upon this joyful termination of the national struggle, Mr. Campbell, by request, delivered to the freemen of East Greenwich, the following address.

" Animated with the liveliest sensibility on the happiness of my country, and pleased with the opportunity of attempting to afford a momentary satisfaction, permit me, gentlemen, to address you.— From merit, rank, or experience, I claim no title to be heard. Let the pleasing influence of the occasion, and the desire to gratify my friends be my only apology. The period hath at length arrived, which we have long anticipated, and hitherto wished for without success. It comes fraught with the last of blessings, the definitive treaty, which is to complete our felicity as a nation, and secure freedom and independence to unborn millions. We have convened; we have heard the enrapturing sound—the voice of peace. She has hushed the savage yell of war, and stayed the ruthless hand of desolation—she hath rewarded our toils and perils —she hath given us liberty.   Under her influence our country will wear a lovelier aspect—our harvests will increase—our fields will be clothed with richer verdure, and commerce waft our products to remoter shores.   Religion will enjoy a more tranquil state, and justice assume a milder form., Oh! Liberty, thou offspring of Heaven, thou dearest friend of man.   Under thy prolific rays the human heart expands to all the social virtues; under thy protection the useful arts are cultivated, and the mind assumes it native dignity, and in unrestrained vigor it launches forth and opens fields of science hitherto unexplored.   O! Liberty, thou nurse of humanity—thou *alma mata* of arts and seiences—may America ever share thy smiles; may this be thy favorite land.   Having reached the haven of security, it may not be unpleasing, perhaps to review the perils, the fatigues and the anxieties we have passed.   This will afford us the satisfaction of contrasted enjoyment—this will learn us to prize our present felicity.   Great Britain, deaf to the voice of justice, and the cry of injured innocence, and determined at every hazard to enforce her oppressive system, transported her conquering veterans—veterans, who had acquired glory on the plains of Abraham.   Yet far from being intimidated by the fame of her achievements, with an invincible love of freedom, undisciplined and unprovided, you cheerfully left your habitations, your friends and valuable endearments; left them not wishing to return, until you might enjoy them unmolested, 'till you should extirpate the foe or perish in the attempt. Under the auspices of your illustrious chief, you have suffered the vicissitudes of war, borne its fatigues, braved its dangers, have fought, bled and conquered. Through every stage of its progress, East Greenwich hath stood unrivalled. When we consider the early and decisive part she took, the unanimity and exertions of her inhabitants, the number and ability of her officers, we shall conceive her entitled to a splendid page in the annals of the revolution; and should she now pursue her advantages in commerce with that spirit and perseverance with which she hath followed freedom, her eminence in retirement would equal her glory in the field. Since we have, with difficulty, obtained the object of our pursuit—since we have risen to empire, with advantages of which no nation anterior to us could boast, let us endeavor to establish our government on the firmest basis, and never tarnish our glory by wielding the rod of oppression. Let our country be renowned for humanity, and afford an asylum to the oppressed of the earth. Then will the nations bless us—then will our felicity equal our power. The savage tones which our minds had acquired by being familiar-

12*

ized to scenes of barbarity are at length relaxed, and a passage opened for the finer feelings of the soul.

Let us, therefore, with hearts replete with gratitude to the Supreme Disposer of events, retire and give scope to those effusions of joy, which the horrors of past distress, or the uncertainty of future events have till now suppressed."

Mr. Campbell having had but little practice in his profession, indulged his native propensity and taste for the muses.   He published a small volume entitled, " Poetical Essays."   To what extent, and with what success this talent was cultivated, the following pieces, which found a place in a well known school book, " The Speaker," will demonstrate.

ON AUTUMN.

Now Sol to southern climes retiring slow
Pursues his annual course, while his
Oblique beams shed but a feeble heat
On this our distant world, and nature all
Around puts on a shady hue.   Far o'er
The dusky mountains east, in sober mantle
Clad, see Autumn comes; smiling she trips
Along, prompt to dispense her bounteous
Gifts, and glads the peasant's heart.   The yellow
Fields with waving grain mature, invite the
Sturdy swains; anon with rustic song and
Soul elate, they ply the cheerful work, soon

As the dawn appears, ere yet the sun has
Gilt the eastern hills; 'till he the horizon
Quits, and evening shades prevail. When home
Returned, the spacious ring is formed, and
Each recounts in conversation free, the
Labors of the day, no recreation
Else, till harvest in. Then pleasure toil
Succeeds, and joy and mirth abound. The jocund
Hours glide unperceived away. The village
Filled with every rural sport,—contention,
Dire and pinching want no more are heard,
But peace and plenty smile around the land.

LIBERTY.

Sweet Liberty! descend thou Heaven born fair,
And make Columbia thy distinguish'd care;
On her brave sons thy genial influence shed,
Who fired by thee have nobly fought and bled—
Have traversed wilds to distant climes afar,
And felt the horrors of oppressive war.
Who first have taught Britannia's troops to yield,
And snatched their standards from the crimsoned field.
Bright Goddess leave thy native skies once more,
And fix thy dwelling on this western shore;
A calm assylum here's prepared for thee,
Secured from tyrants, undisturbed and free;—
By thine assistance we've expell'd thy foes,
Whose grasping power annoyed thy sweet repose.

Lo, see her quit the blissful realms above,
Mark on her face the cheering smile of love;
See as she bends her winged course this way
A beauteous sight her snowy robes display;
In her right hand a sceptered wand she rears,
And in her left a cone-like mitre bears.
Now let us shout through this exulting band,
And hail her welcome to our joyful land.
Let the glad tidings through our coasts resound,
From rocks and mountains let the echo bound,

Let hills and vallies loud responses raise,
Let woods and forests ring in loftier praise,—
Fair Freedom we with joy confess thy sway,
Thy milder laws with pleasure we obey.

To this she listened with attentive ear,
Then spake in accents soft as vernal air :—
"I 've discord seen thy country long embroil,
Thy virtuous struggles and laborious toil ;
Thy valor now I amply will repay
With brighter sunshine and serener day—
The richest blessings which you here can know,
I now on thee and thine unborn bestow.
In future days thy sons shall read thy fame,
Applaud thy conduct and extol thy name,
Throughout the world, in every foreign clime,
Thy deeds shall live down to remotest time—
'Till stars dissolve, and sun and moon expire,
'Till systems burst and nature sink in fire,
My empire here 'till then shall fix'd remain,
'Till then America shall own my reign."

Commerce again now rules the swelling deep,
Her num'rous fleets the surging billows sweep ;
Those stately oaks which lately graced the plain,
In lofty ships now skim the liquid main.
On ev'ry sea, near every kingdom coast,
And bring from thence what they peculiar boast.
Along the strand where flowing tides arise,
See tow'ring cities fix the astonish'd eyes.
Religion here in milder forms array'd,
There Victress Science haunts the laurel shade—
Here culture o'er the fertile earth prevails,
There joy unrivall'd every heart regales.
While this blest region free from dire alarms,
Invites the stranger to her peaceful arms.
With willing hand, she opes her plenteous store,
Relieves his wants, and lets him want no more,—
Grants him a refuge from the despot's chain,
Affords him life, and bids him live again.

Besides the small volume of " Poetical Essays," Mr. Campbell was the author of a number of essays in prose, and some letters which were in existence a few years since, in the hands of a relative. Upon enquiry, he stated that upon his frequent removals, these, with other papers, were so troublesome, that to relieve himself of the burthen, he had burnt them. " In person," says a correspondent, " he was tall, slender and genteel, had a beautiful head of hair, and reputed one of the handsomest men of the day." Elegies were written upon the death of Campbell and of Miss Russell, —they shared the fate of " the other papers."

When disenthralled from the influence of melancholy, Campbell enraptured every circle with the sprightliness of his fancy, and the fascination of his genius. His conversation was rich, his language vivid, style lofty, accompanied by a captivating sweetness that went directly to the heart; but when mentally depressed, he was silent and retiring, and disposed to pour into the bosom of some intimate friend the murmurings of his fancied griefs.

During his residence in college, he became attached to Miss Eliza Russell, daughter of Joseph Russell. Their attachment, growing out of a long friendship, was mutual. He had but a slender and feeble constitution, and was consumptively inclined.

During his lingering confinement, she was constantly with him, and with her own hand ministered to
the object of her plighted love, and her delicate at-
tentions and watchfulness were unceasing. His
sickness was dubious and flattering for a long period ; and she continued her affectionate efforts
for his restoration with unremitted devotion, sometimes buoyed up with the anticipations of a speedy
recovery, at others despairing of a hopeful termination.   If she could not arrest disease, she could
assuage its pains, and with a holy affection smooth
the pillow of death, pluck out its thorns, and
pour upon his soul the healing consolations of the
gospel. After his decease and funeral, she retired to her room and darkened it to her feelings, ad-
mitting only a few select friends, and particularly
those who could discourse of *him*, and like her of
old, refused to be comforted; she remained there
until her death.   A lady of East Greenwich, now
living, who had been intimate with them both,
called to see her, and was admitted to her chamber with scarcely light enough to distinguish an
object.   Her whole conversation was of the sickness, suffering and death of Campbell. She was
awaiting with a patient resignation the arrival of
the wished for hour when she should be summoned
from earth to join him in Heaven.

    She caused handsome tombstones, as the last
tribute of affection, to be erected at his grave, in

the Baptist burial ground, in East Greenwich, next to his father's, with this inscription:

IN MEMORY OF

JACOB CAMPBELL,

SON OF ARCHIBALD CAMPBELL,

ATTORNEY AT LAW,

WHO DEPARTED THIS LIFE MARCH 5TH, 1788, IN THE

28TH YEAR OF HIS AGE.

"Oh faithful Memory may thy lamp illume
The sacred sepulchre with radiance clear,
Soft plighted love shall rest upon his tomb,
And friendship o'er it shed the fragrant tear."

The suicidal course adopted by this unfortunate young lady, upon this eventful occasion, should not be allowed to pass without reproof. The dispensations of Heaven, however severe, are to be met and borne with christian resignation. The infliction of self injury or immolation, proceeds upon a principal of retaliation or revenge, utterly at variance with every feature of the Christian character; and must impress the conviction that its doctrines must have been defectively inculcated, or grossly misunderstood. That she should have wept, and bitterly have wept to be bereaved of the object of her tenderest affections; that her wounded heart should have heaved with the deepest emotions upon their earthly separation, is what all would expect, and in which all would sympathize. But to incarcerate her person, and prematurely terminate her existence, that Providence, in its visitations, had disappointed her hopes, all must equally condemn.

JAMES MITCHELL VARNUM.

Two brothers, of the name of Varnum, emigrated from Wales to Boston, just prior to the year 1660, and from thence to Ipswich, where one died without issue. Samuel, the survivor, purchased a large tract of land of the Indians, in the town of Dracut, county of Middlesex, Massachusetts, and settled on it in 1664. He had issue, five sons, John, Thomas and Joseph, and two who were shot in a boat while crossing the Merrimack with their father. The descendants of John and Thomas reside in Dracut and elsewhere. Joseph was colonel of the militia, and was wounded in the Indian war of 1676. He erected a garrison house, which is still standing as the family mansion, in a good state of preservation. Joseph Varnum left two sons, Joseph and Samuel, who inherited a large estate from their father. Joseph had issue, and several families have descended from him. Samuel had four sons, Samuel, James Mitchell, Joseph Bradley and Daniel Varnum. Samuel died in Maine about twenty years since. Joseph B. in 1821, and Daniel in 1822, on the patrimonial estate, which has remained in the family since the first purchase from

13

the natives.   Most of the brothers held prominent
official stations in Massachusetts.   Joseph B. was
elected a member of Congress from his native district in 1795, and successively re-elected till 1811,
and then elected Senator one term, making his
whole service in Congress twenty-two years.   From
1807 to 1811, comprising two congressional terms,
he was elected Speaker of the House of Representatives.

The subject of this memoir, James Mitchell Varnum, was born in Dracut, the residence of his ancestors, in 1749.   He entered Rhode-Island College, now Brown University, then established in
Warren, and was in the first class that graduated
from that institution, in 1769, at the age of twenty.
He received the first honors of his class, and in a
forensic discussion vindicated the rights of the colonies in their resistance to British taxation, with
signal ability.   He kept a classical school for a
short period after he graduated, and always spoke
highly of its benefits to a student, to plant deeply
on the mind those elements acquired in the college
hall; and his whole life demonstrated that he had
profited by it.   He was deeply attached to mathe-
matical science, and delighted in its pursuit;—his
whole life was an evidence that he was naturally a
mathematician—his habits were those of intense
study and boisterous relaxation.   " He was fond of

exhibiting his skill in gymnastics, and ever ready to exercise in that ancient art with any one who would engage with him, noble or ignoble. Strong and active in frame, and ardently attached to such exercises, he gave his inclination for such sports the fullest range to a late period of his life."

Soon after his college course, he entered the office of Oliver Arnold, in Providence, then Attorney General of the colony. William Channing, Thomas Arnold, John S. Dexter, and himself, were students together at the time of Mr. Arnold's death, in 1770, and in the succeeding year Varnum was admitted to the bar. He settled at East Greenwich, where his talents acquired for him an extensive practice; and he travelled the circuits of the state reaping the honors and rewards of his profession.

Mr. Varnum had a great taste for military life, and early joined the "Kentish Guards," and was appointed commander of that company in 1774— a company, which from their acquirements in military tactics, became the nursery of so many distinguished officers during the revolutionary war. Gen. Greene, Gen. Varnum, Col. Greene, Col. Crary, Major Whitmarsh, and others, making thirty-two in all, who entered the revolutionary army, as commissioned officers, from this company alone. The

prominent part Mr. Varnum had taken in the colonial controversy, inspired an ambition to enter the
military service of his country. The venerable
John Howland, President of the Historical Society of
this state, in a communication, states, that " when
the news of the Lexington battle reached East
Greenwich, Varnum's company mustered and
marched to Providence, on their way to the scene
of action. I recollect seeing them on their arrival.
Nathaniel Greene, of Coventry, afterwards the
General, was a private with a musket on his shoulder, and Christopher Greene, afterwards Colonel
Greene, who defended Red Bank, was also there,
a private in the same company. They marched beyond Pawtucket, and hearing that the enemy had
retired to Boston, they returned. The next week
the General Assembly convened, and resolved to
raise three regiments of infantry and a company
of artillery. Mr. Nathaniel Greene, then a member of the House of Representatives, was appointed Brigadier General, and Varnum, Colonel of the
regiment to be raised in the counties of Kent and
Kings. Daniel Hitchcock to be Colonel of the regiment to be raised in Providence, and Church to be
Colonel of the regiment to be raised in the counties of Newport and Bristol. Varnum took rank
over Hitchcock and Church, from having commanded in the ' Kentish Guards,' with the rank of
Colonel. The time for which these troops were

called out expired December 31, 1775. The state raised two regiments for the year 1776. Varnum commanded the first, and Hitchcock the second. The officers of these troops afterwards received commissions from the President of Congress, when Washington was appointed commander-in-chief. They were then styled continental troops. In January, 1776, the state raised a regiment called state troops, to be stationed in New-port. They remained there until the disastrous battle on Long Island. This regiment command ed by Col. Lippitt, was taken into the continental service, and ordered to join Gen. Washington at New York; they arrived at Haerlem after the evacuation of the city. This regiment composed part of the brigade commanded by Gen. John Nixon, which consisted of five regiments, commanded by Col's. Nixon and Little, of Massachusetts, Varnum, Hitchcock and Lippett, of Rhode-Island. Towards the close of the year, Gen. Nixon was dispatched by the commander-in-chief, on furlough, to Massachusetts, to urge the raising of new recruits for the army to supply the place of those whose term of service would expire on the 31st of December, as without reinforcements Gen. Washington would be left without an army at the commencement of the succeeding year. Gen. Varnum then succeeded to the command of the brigade. But the necessity of the case, and the perilous situation of the

13*

country induced Gen. Washington soon after to send Gen. Varnum to the Assembly of Rhode-Island for the same purpose. Selecting for this all important mission these officers for their known influence with their respective legislatures. The command of this brigade of five regiments then devolved on Colonel Hitchcock, as the senior officer. And he commanded it at a period the most important in our revolutionary history, and led his brigade with courage and ability in the memorable battles of Trenton and Princetown, and for his signal gallantry received the special thanks of Gen. Washington, in front of the college at Princeton, and which he was requested to present to the brigade he had so ably commanded. " You may ask," continues Mr. Howland, " why I have recited this long piece of old history, when the subject on which I am engaged is merely a notice of Varnum, as a Rhode-Island lawyer, to which I reply, that his military history is so intimately connected with his civil pursuits, that they cannot be properly separated. And in this detail, Varnum and Hitchcock, as two Rhode-Island lawyers, reflect no small honor on the Rhode-Island bar."

In February, 1777, Col. Varnum was promoted by Congress to the rank of Brigadier General.— The appointment was announced to him by Gen. Washington by letter under date of March 3d, of that year, which contains ample evidence that his military bearing had met the full approbation of the commander-in-chief. The General Assembly of this state, at their December session, 1776, having appointed General Varnum commander of the state forces, at their March session, 1777, entered the following honorable testimonial of approbation on their legislative journal : " Whereas the appointment and commission of Brigadier General James M. Varnum in the service of this state has been suspended by his being appointed by the Hon. Continental Congress to the same rank in the continental army, this Assembly do therefore, in grateful remembrance of his services, *vote and resolve,* that he is dismissed from his said appointment, and that he be paid to the time his pay commenced in the continental service." " Under the latter appointment," continues Mr. Howland, " Gen. Varnum commanded all that body of troops on the Jersey side of the Delaware, when the British and Hessians took possession of Philadelphia. General Washington's purpose was to prevent the passage of the enemy's shipping up the river, and for this purpose a strong fort was erected on Red Bank, and a battery on Mud Island. The two Rhode-Island regiments were stationed at Red Bank, and a regiment of Marylanders on Mud Island. Colonel Christopher Greene commanded the two Rhode-Island regiments, Lieut. Col. Samuel Smith on Mud Island, and Varnum the whole line of the coast in New Jersey. In October the enemy made a determined attack, but the battery and fort were so valiantly defended, that the invaders were defeated and compelled to withdraw, and temporarily to abandon the enterprize. The gallant defence of fort Mifflin, or Mud Island, and the defeat of the Hessians at fort Mercer, or Red Bank, drew from Congress, then sitting at Yorktown, a resolution of thanks, and votes of elegant swords to Col. Greene, Lieut. Col. Smith and Commodore Hazlewood, for their intrepid defence of these two forts.*   But the British resolved on the capture of these posts, so important in their position, renewed the attack in November. They brought up their shipping—the Somersett, of sixty-four guns, and a number of floating batteries to break up the *chevaux de frise* which extended across the river, and our forts opened their fire to prevent it." Colonel Smith was wounded on the 11th of November, and the command devolved upon Lieut. Col. Russell, of the Connecticut line, who exhausted by fatigue and destitute of health, requested to be recalled. The moment was critical. The commander-in-chief, Gen. Washington, had no idea of defending the place through the campaign, but wished to retard the operations of the enemy, until the main army should be reinforced by the Massachusetts brigade marching

---

*See Appendix, No. 5.

from the conquest at Saratoga, when he would be in sufficient force to cover the country or meet the enemies whole force in the field. Upon the 12th, he signified his wish to Gen. Varnum to defend the island as long as possible, without sacrificing the garrison. General Varnum considering the imminent danger of the post, immediately convened the field officers of Red Bank fort, with a request that one of them would volunteer, as Gen. Washington desired the Island to be defended as long as possible, and take command of it in lieu of Smith, who had left. At this momentous crisis, Major Simeon Thayer immediately offered himself, to the inexpressible satisfaction of Gen. Varnum. In the defence, to an officer knowing all the circumstances, nothing presented itself but death, or an improbable escape, without the possibility of contending on even terms. But Major Thayer gallantly defended it day and night from the 12th to 12 o'clock on the night of the 16th of November, when the breastworks were beaten down, and no cover was left for his men, when the General ordered him to abandon it. By those unacquainted with the transaction, all the glory has been ascribed to Col. Smith. If heroic valor was to be rewarded, who should have had a sword? When the swords, which were wrought in France, arrived, and were to be presented, Gen. Varnum published a letter, dated at East Greenwich, Au-

gust 3d, 1786,* narrating all the circumstances àt-
tending the heroic defence of Mud Island by Major
Thayer. It is written in a natural and straight-
forward style, and in justice to the memory of this
intrepid soldier of Rhode-Island, and of his country,
ought to be preserved in some durable form.

General Varnum continued in active service during the year 1778, and commanded a brigade in
Sullivan's expedition on Rhode-Island. In 1779,
he resigned his commission in the army, there being, at that time, more general officers in the service than were needful in proportion to the men,
and his talents too being more congenial with political life than the duties of the camp, although he
was respected and esteemed as a good and gallant
officer.

The Legislature of this state, in consideration
of Gen. Varnum's national services, and effectually
to secure them in defence of the state, in May,
1779, elected him Major General of the militia of
the state, to which office he was unanimously re-
elected during the remainder of his life. In April,
1780, the people of the state, in grateful recollection of his eminent services in the cause of public
liberty, and desirous to throw into the national
councils those distinguished talents which could be

---

* See Appendix, No. 6.

spared from the field, elected him their delegate to the confederated Congress of that year. As that body sat with closed doors, his voice could not be heard by the public, but his name appears oftener on the published journals than many others of that body.

The following letter from Gen. Varnum to John Innis Clarke, of Providence, gives a faithful and vivid picture of the situation and condition of the United States and its finances, the inefficiency of the confederation, the necessity of an energetic constitution; a well formed National bank, and the deplorable evils resulting from the paper money system, with a bird's eye view of the tardy movements of the magnates of the great Council house of the union.

PHILADELPHIA, Feb'y 3d, 1781.

Sir,—This evening gives me leisure to write to you freely, and as far as I am able to judge, fully, of the important concerns of the United States. As many are of opinion that my predecessor was too communicative, my letters to the Governor have been dictated by caution, though containing general truths.

I lament with the most serious inquietude, the contents of this letter, but as they are dictated by the clearest conviction, you have my cordial approbation in making them known either to a select circle, or the legislature, as your discretion may direct.

From the first period of the depreciation of the continental currency, the cords of government were relaxed; and with the rapidity of the former the latter has kept pace. All expedients, such as fixing prices, making tender laws, and laying embargoes, instead of alleviating, materially increased the evil. Congress in order to make one great effort towards reducing the public debt, and restoring public credit, on the 18th March last made the resolve of sinking the old, and emitting new bills. Their intentions, I mean the intentions of the majority, were undoubtedly good, but if a plan can be judged of by its effects, they could not have adopted one more fatal to the great objects they had in contemplation. Its operations have been various in the different states. Some accepted it readily; some with delay, and others not at all. The consequences were, there was no money in the treasury. Creditors grew uneasy; credit was stretched upon vague promises, without a possibility of performance; the army unpaid as it had been for more than a year—unclothed and unfed, and therefore mutinous. The requisitions upon the states for specific supplies were owing to the want of money, and these supplies have been as uncertain as the measure was impolitic and unjust, as it would necessarily make some states lenders to others without the consent of the former. Indeed, sir, we have neither money to pay the interest of our debt, nor credit enough to contract new ones. We are destitute of every requisite for the ensuing campaign, and have it not in our power to extricate ourselves from such an alarming situation, while we know from the surest information that Great Britain is exerting every nerve to make the most decisive operations. Notwithstanding these really distressing circumstances, the country abounds with resources. Every article of provision is in the greatest plenty; dry goods are by no means scarce, and West India produce is very cheap. Pennsylvania alone has more grain and flour this moment, exclusive of what would suffice the inhabitants, than is sufficient for an army of fifty thousand men, for the term of a year. Money is by no means scarce. It is true, the fluctuating circumstances of the paper currency may have made its circulation unequal, but still it is in the country, and if there is not specie, there is plate enough to make up every deficiency. Our perplexities do not arise from poverty, or the want of men, but from the absolute want of government. It is a fact as demonstrable as any proposition in Euclid, that when a number of sovereign, independent states are mutually engaged in war, neither of them is adequate to any of its conclusive purposes. Hence

14

the necessity of a federal union, by which the wisdom, the virtue, the strength and resources of the
whole may be conjointly centered and exerted.
In this fundamental principle, however, we fail.
For it is notorious that Congress have not the
power of calling forth the resources of the country.
It is probable, I confess, that the confederation will
be concluded; but then we shall be just where we
are now, in a perfect state of imbecility. By the
act of confederation Congress is not vested with
powers requisite in the time of war. They are authorized to make war or peace, but they are not
competent to the means of supporting either. Suppose they call upon the states for money or supplies, and some of them neglect or refuse, as they
invariably do, where is the power of compulsion?
And without that it is evident the best measures
may be frustrated. We have stumbled upon expedients too long; we have too long trifled with objects of the greatest magnitude; we have trusted
to Heaven for success to our arms, while we have
neglected to improve the means with which the
God of nature has blessed us. Among confederated
states there must be a supreme control, equally effective upon all. I am confident from observation,
history and reflection, that the present war will
never be carried on with success 'till Congress or
some other body are invested by the States with
all the power necessary to command the resources

of the country. Trade and commerce, those great sources of national wealth, should undoubtedly be subject to exact regulation; but if each state should undertake the matter separately, every gentleman of common understanding will readily perceive the confusion and innumerable frauds, relatively to each other and to individuals, that must result. Congress, therefore, should be intrusted with the power of laying duties, by which the United States would derive a considerable revenue. If they could once command a certain permanent revenue, national credit would be restored, and large sums could be borrowed on the faith of a bank which might easily be established. Those modes only of drawing money into the national treasury, which are least felt, and of consequence the most satisfactory to the people at large, should be adopted. Industry is the most obvious source of wealth, and indeed without its being generally encouraged, commerce itself must cease; taxes must cease, and war must cease by terminating in conquest. The fewer the embarrassments therefore which are thrown on the people the better; they should always have a sure market for their labor, and certain pay. To this end embargoes should never be tolerated but upon the most pressing occasion, such as the investiture of a place, where the siege may probably be turned into a blockade. Of the necessity of which the general Congress or the com-

mander-in-chief, on the spot, should be the judge
in time of war.   In peace, perhaps, the case might
be different.   Hence expectations of every kind,
excepting articles where there is a real scarcity,
should be encouraged.   From policy like this we
should find all discontents removed.   The citizens
would feel reiterated spirit and vigour; wealth
would be diffused in abundance, and the means of
government rendered familiar, and by no means
burthensome.   I will suppose, for a moment, that
the expenses for the current year will amount to
twenty millions of dollars, including the arrearages
of the army's pay; the interest upon loan office
certificates and foreign debts, exclusive of the expenses of each particular state for supporting its
own internal police, where is the sum to come
from ?—The new money, supposing it to be productive, which I don't believe but in part, is equal to
only half its nominal value in specie.   The continent therefore would gain only five millions of dollars; little is to be expected from requisitions upon
the states, for some collect their taxes slowly, and
some not at all.   If we rely upon a loan from
France we shall be deceived, for the minister of
France will reason in this way.   France and the
United States are conjointly engaged in a war with
Great Briain; it is necessary for the good of both
the allies that as great a force as possible should
be exerted against the common enemy, but the

quantity of this force depends on the ways and means of both countries, and the manner in which they are applied. Now it is evident that with the same sum of money, France can exert treble the force that America can under the present impolitic systems. Therefore, the minister will very rationally conclude that to lend the United States money will equally injure them and France. From whence then are we to obtain the fifteen millions? I acknowledge that such an immense sum cannot be collected in the course of a year; no country is able to carry on war with taxation, or any other mode of collecting money from individuals in an equal ratio. But there is an easy way of making six millions represent twenty, which turns ultimately into an internal debt, that is where a bank is well formed, notes may issue to a large amount, and when the holders find that they can receive their real money by applying to the bank, they will soon give over the trouble of exchanging, as they become fully confident in the security, and find paper of a light carriage. Whenever paper represents money, it is valued nearly in proportion to the substance, but the misfortune of our paper has been that it represents real estate, and all the articles of living, without being funded upon any thing substantial. It is well known that the real cash of Great Britain amounts to no more than

14*

eight millions sterling, yet their circulating medi•
um in notes, inland bills, &c. is immense. The
same takes place in France, Holland and all the
trading nations. We certainly can effect the
same, but different councils will always produce
different systems, and these systems will, of course,
destroy each other. Therefore the powers of revenue must be in one body throughout the union.
I hope Congress will send to the states, in a very
short time, some plan by which they may be invested with proper authority. But in this idea I am
exceedingly mortified, and indeed vexed to the last
degree. A plan of revenue has been before them,
and dwelt upon nearly three weeks, and upon my
honor they have made no greater progress than a
man of sense would have done in three hours; but,
you will say, the delays of deliberative councils are
a natural sacrifice that civil society must make to
obtain an excellent political form of government.
True, but our delays are infinitely greater than
they need be. There are a certain number of
members who have been in Congress a long time,
and think themselves possessed of all knowledge.
A question cannot be started, however trivial, but
they make formal speeches, for fear the young
members should misconceive the subject, and if the
matter, as that just mentioned, should be of amazing consequence, much more time is thought necessary to properly enforce it. But if it requires im-

mediate dispatch, then great deliberation is essentially requisite. There are some who make their ideas the standards of all judgments; and if a particular word in a report should not exactly suit their mechanical geniuses a long debate ensues. I assure you sir, they often make me think of Neal's history of the Puritans, in which the speeches made in the long Parliament are recorded at length. And I have not failed to tell them upon the floor that their fate will be similar to that of the former, unless they pursue different modes and means. In matters of this consequence, I mean when the revenue is in serious question, the Duke de Tully tells us every moment taken up in debate is lost, and probably may never be recalled. A Titus could weep that he had lost a day, but we, I am almost constrained to say it, have lost years. I now come to the conclusion; if Congress is not speedily vested with adequate powers for commanding the means for carrying on the war with energy, and if they do not exert those properly, a few months will put an end to their existence. What kind of administration will succeed God only knows. I have one consolation however, that we shall not be conquered by Great Britain; the people will not suffer it, but our calamities may be inexpressibly augmented by such a change. While I continue here, I shall spare no pains of body or mind to serve my country, but I am determined to acquit myself

in the eyes of God and man of any fatal consequences that may attend our public measures.

I might write Governor Bowen and several other
gentlemen, but I can say no more than this letter
contains, and I believe you will be sufficiently fa-
tigued in reading it. My best respects to all friends.

I am Sir, with every sentiment of esteem, your
obedient, and most humble servant,

J. M. VARNUM.

Mr. Clarke.

Mr. Howland continues to observe,—"The old
Congress under the confederation had no power to
raise money to carry on the war, either by taxes
or imposts, and the states had enough to do to furnish their own treasuries. Congress, on the third
of February, 1781, requested the several states to
grant them power to levy an impost at five per
cent. ad valorem on all imported goods and all
prizes and prize goods, to be appropriated to the
discharge of the principal and interest of the debts
contracted, or to be contracted on the faith of the
United States, for the supporting of the war. This
was thought necessary for the salvation of the
country, and to maintain our independence. The
granting of this power to Congress to raise a revenue was a new question, and divided the politicians in its discussion. To place the case in its

urgent necessity before the respective legislatures
of the states, several of the best speakers in Congress were requested, or thought proper to return
home and persuade the people to grant the power.
Rufus King advocated it in Massachusetts, Dayton
left his seat to advance the cause in New Jersey,
and Varnum came to Rhode-Island for the same
purpose. The states which had little or no maritime commerce, readily granted the power. This
question brought a new man into the field in Rhode-
Island. David Howell, knowing the importers
would generally oppose the power, and that the
people at large would unwillingly be deprived of a
rich source of state revenue, at a crisis so distressing, came out in the Providence Gazette, and in all
public places, with violent declamation against the
" FIVE PER CENT.," as it was called. He argued if
you once grant them FIVE they will soon take TEN,
then TWENTY, &c. General Varnum vindicated
the grant, in the same paper, over the signature of
" CITIZEN." Howell over that of " FARMER," knowing the majority of every state were farmers. At
length the question came before the General Assembly. Varnum's speech occupied the forenoon,
and in strength of argument and eloquence had
not been equalled since the settlement of the state.
Howell occupied the afternoon; the question was
then taken, and decided in the negative. It was

afterwards ascertained that a majority had prede-
termined and agreed not to grant the power."*

"Under the confederation, no state could be represented by less than two, nor more than seven
representatives in Congress, and as they voted by
states and not by numbers, Rhode-Island sent but
two, as each state had to pay its own members.
Howell was elected in the place of Varnum, and
Jonathan Arnold, [the father of Gov. Lemuel H.
Arnold,] in the place of Ellery. Eleven of the
states granted the "*five per cent.*" New York,
headed by George Clinton, never decided one way
or the other, and Rhode-Island refused." So Congress were defeated in the necessary source of revenue, all the states not concurring in the measure.

After the war Gen. Varnum recommenced the
practice of law at East Greenwich, with increased
reputation, and was promptly engaged in all the
important causes in the state. At that period great
and important cases arose growing out of the new
position in which the state and nation were placed.

---

* This controversy between Varnum and Howell afterwards assumed a personal character. Varnum published
a parody on Howell, who in return published a soliloquy
on Varnum. They afterwards became reconciled, and
were friends.

The great case of Trevett *vs*. Weeden was one
which stirred the community to its very foundation.
Upon its issue was involved the destiny of thousands. Public feeling and anxiety were intense
upon its result. The period succeeding the revolution was the most eventful in our history. The
crisis arose, and the experiment was on trial,
whether the people were capable of self government; and upon its issue depended the fate of the
nation. The country was exhausted by a protracted contest, and disappointed in the expectation of
sufficient national resources to meet the embarrassments produced by it, insubordination and misrule
showed themselves every where. The army returned unpaid and discontented, with certificates upon a
bankrupt treasury, instead of money, amidst a state
population as impoverished as themselves. The
state itself was insolvent and wholly unable to pay
the bills of credit against it. The stock of the farmer was selling at the auction posts for the payment
of taxes. The old Congress was as embarrassed
as the states for pecuniary means to discharge their
engagements. They made requisitions in conformity to the powers delegated to them under the articles of confederation. Owing to inability the states
rejected them. The bills which Congress had ne-
gociated in Holland for the payment of the army
were unpaid at maturity, and returned protested.
The damages alone amounting to the startling sum

of six hundred and thirty-six thousand dollars. At this act of sovereign dishonor and disgrace of the new republic, our ambassadors, Franklin, Jay and Adams were in despair. Prompted by exorbitant profit, the merchants shipped to Europe all the remaining specie that could be obtained, to supply the country with fabrics which the war had exhausted. Massachusetts alone exported three millions of specie from the commencement of peace to July, 1785, and we can only judge, by estimation, of the vast amount exported from other seaports for the like purposes. So that in a short period all the gold brought by the French, and the silver imported from the Spanish West Indies, was drained from the country. The avaricious course pursued by the merchants compelled the borrower to pay *twenty* per cent. per annum, and some *four* per cent. per month. Such was the posture of affairs at this momentuous crisis. The confederation was powerless. The veteran soldiery who had exposed themselves to tempests and battles through the whole contest, and whom peace had dismissed with laurels, returned to their families penniless and clamorous. The community was in a thraldom. Necessity and distress showed themselves by insurrections and commotions in every quarter. If Shays had possessed courage equal to his address and ability, he might have marched in triumph through the nation, gathering to his standard dis-

affected spirits enough to have insured him victory—such was the perilous condition of the republic. The mercantile mania for exporting the precious metals from the country, united the farmer,
the tax-payer, the debtor and the borrower with
remorseless acrimony against them, as the authors
of their sufferings. Spirits enough are always con-
jured up at such a crisis, who are ready to gratify
their ambition and other still more sinister motives.
The state threw itself upon its reserved rights.—
And the demagogues who could best live and flour-
ish in turbulent political waters, seizing upon the
agitated occasion, with Jonathan J. Hazard at their
head, roused the distressed of every class into a
phrenzy, and made them believe that, Midas like,
they could touch paper and convert it to gold.
They were thus goaded into this false, this fatal
step. The paper money party obtained an overwhelming majority, and expressly instructed their
representatives for the purpose. With a " paper
money" Senate, and Gov. Collins at its head, the
General Assembly, in May, 1786, emitted the enormous sum of £100,000 in paper bills. Committees
were elected to sign and distribute them to the
towns in proportion to their population. It was
further enacted that said bills, when emitted, should
be " a good and lawful tender for the complete payment and final discharge of all fines, forfeitures,

judgments, and executions that had become due and recovered of every kind and nature whatsoever" And it then further provided the mode of making said tender effectual in law. It will be observed, that there was no time fixed when said bills were to be redeemed, nor was their ultimate payment charged upon any fund; nor was it designated how they were to be paid. But on the contrary they were to be loaned for fourteen years upon mortgage *pro rata,* to all the people, at four per cent. interest for the first seven years, and to be repaid in the next seven years by the mortgagees in seven equal installments, without interest; and then they were "*to be consumed by fire.*" Thus intending to annihilate the merchants, their fancied opponents, at a blow. But as it might have been expected, these bills fell into immediate discredit. Those who had property chose rather to retain than exchange it.

The paper money party, (for the *whig and tory* of the revolution were at this period commuted into the *hard and paper money* parties,) were exasperated at defeat, and indignant at the rejection of their promised specific. Their leaders, at the June session succeeding, thundered another legislative anathema against their *hard money* opponents, by an additional enactment, stating in the preamble, " that it was of the greatest moment that the aforesaid emission of £100,000, which had the greatest tendency of any thing within the wisdom of the legislature, to quiet the minds and alleviate the distressed situation and circumstances of the good citizens of this state, should be kept in good credit, and that the same should be a currency equal in value to *coined* gold and silver. And whereas various attempts have been made by A CERTAIN CLASS OF MEN, who from mistaken principles suppose the said currency to be injurious to their interests, and from an inclination to render invalid such laws and regulations of this Assembly as might not graduate with their interests, judgment and opinion of things, and for many other causes, which if permitted to exist, will support a power in this state counter to the authority chosen and appointed by the free suffrages of the people thereof, and subversive of the laws and principles upon which the happiness, welfare and safety of the people depend," enacted that any person who should refuse to take these bills of credit in exchange for any articles which he may have for sale, according to the amount expressed on the face of said bills, or make any difference in the prices between silver and paper money in any sale or exchange, or direct the same to be done; or in any manner whatever tend or attempt to depreciate or discourage the passing of said bills, of the price of the face thereof, or do any act to invalidate or weaken the said act emit-

ting said bills, for the first offence shall forfeit and
pay the sum of £100, and be rendered incapable
of being elected to any office of honor, trust or
profit within this state."

This additional act, tyrannical and arbitrary as
it was in its provisions, failed in effecting the contemplated remedy. The farmers however were so
ignorant of political economy, and so far influenced
by demagogues as to believe that legislative enact-
ments could transmute paper into gold, and that public confidence could be created in currency by political power, without the immediate certainty that
such currency could be converted into the metal it
was intended to represent. Further, they meant
to wreak their vengeance on the opponents of their
system, and to force by further penalties the reception of their favorite measure of general relief, as
equivalent to gold. Not intending that their political *hobby* should long stand still, or that the public
mind should have time enough to become quiet or
composed, these agitators called a special session of
the legislature in August, of the same year, making
three sessions in four months, mostly spent upon
the Quixotic experiment of transforming paper into
gold by legislative alchymy.

The preamble to the act passed at this last session displays the whole spirit of the paper money
party of that day. It states, " that it is an estab-

lished maxim of legislation, and ought to be strictly
and punctually adhered to in all wise governments,
that process upon the breach of penal laws should
be immediate, and the penalty inflicted or exacted
directly consequent upon conviction. And that the
usual and stated times of holding courts within this
state, are impracticable, inconvenient and inappli-
cable to the true intent and meaning of said act;
and altogether insufficient to carry into effect the
good purposes of this legislature, touching the same."
And it was enacted that if any person refused to
receive said bills as coin, as was before enacted,
the complainant should apply to either of the
Judges of the Supreme or Common Pleas courts,
and citation should be issued to the refusing party
to appear before a special court within three days
and there stand his trial, *without a jury*, according
to the laws of the land, before said court. And
the judgment of said court, upon the conviction of
the accused, was to be forthwith executed, and the
offender immediately to pay said penalty, or stand
committed to jail until sentence should be performed; which said judgment was to be final and conclusive, and without appeal. No delay, protection,
privilege or injunction should, in any case, be prayed for, allowed or granted.

They were not satisfied with the despotism of the
last act, although in the language of Rufus King
15*

upon a different occasion, "its red was as red as blood, and its black as black as Tartarus." Fearing the failure of its expected efficacy, at the same August extra session, a bill passed the House of Representatives, entitled " an act to stimulate and give efficacy to the paper bills issued by the state in May last." This bill was sent out and submitted to the consideration of the freemen at large, in order that they might make known their sentiments respecting the same, at the respective town meetings to be holden in that month, by instructing their representatives elected for the next October session. This bill contained a criminal provision for refusing to take these bills at par with silver and gold. The delinquent was to be ineligible to any post of honor or profit within this state, or to exercise the functions of any civil or military office therein—or to give his vote or suffrage for electing any officer or representative in this state. This amounted at once to a disfranchisement and proscription of all those who differed in opinion from the majority, upon what civil consideration they should part with their private property. And in conclusion, it enacted a test whereby all the freemen of the state, and others, were required to *swear or affirm* that they would use their endeavors to give the paper money, (of this state,) a currency equal to gold and silver, and that they would sell their vendible articles for the same prices for the one as the other." And in the case of failure " were to be punished as for wilful and corrupt perjury."* These last acts are without a parallel in the annals of civilization. But all these measures proved as fruitless as the preceding ones in producing the desired results. These deluded and deluding men held in their hands the fancied cornucopia of wealth and happiness, and wielded at pleasure its promised benefits, and attempted to annihilate by penal legislation all those whom they supposed could wrest it from their grasp. They impressed upon their adherents that they had borne the goadings of want, that they had suffered under the tortures of penury, and in their new discovered *solvent* of transmuting paper into gold, they were rioting in all the luxuries of antici-

---

* Upon the publication of this intended bill, the citizens of Providence called a town meeting to take the contents into consideration. The Hon. Jabez Bowen, Nicholas Brown, Welcome Arnold, John I. Clark and Theodore Foster, were appointed a committee to draught instructions to their representatives in the General Assembly.— Their report is an able document, and worthy of the best days of the republic. They unanimously voted, that John Jenckes, John Brown, Charles Keene, and Benjamin Bourne, Esq'rs., their representatives, be instructed to vote and use all their influence against said projected bill. The report undoubtedly had great influence on the public mind.

pated plenty. They had created their own bank, and could issue their money in countless thousands; they had made laws compelling their bills to be taken as equivalent to gold and silver; they had elected a partizan judicature to carry their laws into execution; they had deprived their opponents of the sacred palladium of Britons, *the trial by jury*, and the freemen who opposed them, of elegibility to office. They had enacted the payment of ruinous penalties, and prescribed an immediate incarceration upon the instant of non-compliance with the judgment of the court. These swollen dictators, and their supporters, were in the full fruition of all their visions,—but the catastrophe was at hand; equity, justice, and the constitution, was on the one side, and power and misrule on the other. Upon the issue of the conflict, the fate of the paper money system, and its partizans, were to stand or fall forever in Rhode-Island.

This paper money narrative may be instructive and novel to some, and a tedious " thrice told tale" to others. Its history is given as far as it is necessarily connected with the trial to be mentioned, in order to bring Gen. Varnum in his strength and eloquence before you, for this was his giant effort.

In September, 1786, the case of Trevett against Weeden arose. John Trevett, of Newport, bought meat of John Weeden, a butcher, in the market, and tendered to him bills of the emission of May preceding, in payment, which Weeden refused. A complaint was made and filed in accordance with the acts of the General Assembly, before Paul Mumford, chief justice of the Supreme Court, at his chambers, who caused a special court to be convened, but as the information was filed during the term, it was referred to the regular sittings of the court for determination under the provisions of the paper money laws.

The defendant pleaded, "that it appears by the act of the General Assembly, wherein said information was founded, that the act had expired, and hath no force. Also, for that by said act the matters of complaint are made triable before special courts uncontrolable by the supreme judiciary court of the state. Also, for that the said court is not, by said act, authorized and empowered to *empannel a jury* to try the facts charged in the information, and so the same is unconstitutional and void."

The Court consisted of
> PAUL MUMFORD, *Chief Justice.*
> JOSEPH HAZARD,
> THOMAS TILLINGHAST, } *Associates.*
> DAVID HOWELL,

The decisive hour had now arrived. If the complaint was sustained by the judgment of the court, the creditor, merchant, farmer, and every vendor was prostrated in utter ruin. In fact, all the commerce and business of the state would be effectually destroyed, and all previous obligations canceled by this irredeemable *trash.* The whole public was under a feverish excitement; the merchant closed his store, the farmers and tenants who depended on sales, left their fields, and the mechanic his workshop, and all congregated at the court house to await the eventful issue.

The paper money politicians and their partizans, not to be behind their opponents, were there in full force and numbers to cheer their friends, and to encourage or overawe their partizan created court. Supported by the influence and array of embarrassed debtors, harrassed by creditors without a currency to pay them, the impoverished landholder distressed by an excessive taxation—his property distrained by the officers of the law. And last, but not least, the state debtors who had just mortgaged their estates for bills under the new emission act. Under all these circumstances, the friends of the complaint were confident of success, and elated with the prospect of a speedy victory.

In this arena, and amid all the impressive circumstances, Gen. Varnum rose to advocate the cause of the defendant. In his opening, he triumphantly lifted himself above his professional vocation. " I do not appear," he said, " may it please the honorable court, on the present occasion, so much in the line of my profession, as in the character· of the citizen deeply interested in the constitutional laws of a free sovereign and independent state. And indeed, whenever the rights of all the citizens appear to be essentially connected with a controverted question, conscious of the dignity of our profession, we exercise our professional talents only as a means conducive to the great ends of political society and general happiness. In this arduous, though pleasing pursuit, should my efforts appear too feeble to support the attempt, I shall derive a consolation in reflectng that the learned and honorable gentleman at my right, [Henry Marchant, Esq.,] is associated with me in the defence."

That there reigned the deepest silence through the multitude during this exordium, we are assured from the following sentence. " Well may a profound silence mark the attention of this numerous and respectable assembly!—Well may anxiety be displayed in every countenance!—Well may the dignity of the bench condescend to our solicitude for a most candid and serious attention, seeing that from the first settlement of this country until the

present moment, a question of such magnitude as
that upon which the judgment of the court is now
prayed, hath not been judicially agitated."

The exordium was both appropriate and beautiful, and well befitting the great occasion upon
which the court were to act so high and responsible a part. We may feel from it, that the orator
soared above the lawyer. The keen attention ex- ·
hibited by the crowded audience, the anxious countenances, the courteous dignity of the bench, in a
moment impress us, that it was the member of
Congress, the General who had bared his bosom
for his country, that now addressed them; lifting
his arm and raising his voice to save that country
in the forum as he had in the field. The lawyer
was forgotten in the statesman, pleading not the
case of the forlorn Weeden, but the cause of a torn
and distracted state.

He happily elevated the court above the tram-
mels of party, and made them feel conscious of the
high responsibility of their situation, and compelled them to feel that they were no longer " paper
money" tools, mechanically to perform the works
of a junto; but robed as judges expounding the
law and the constitution. He continues—

" It is extremely to be regretted that this court

is not as independent in the tenure by which the judges hold their commissions, as they are in the exercise of their judicial proceedings. The frequent changes that arise from annual appointments, may have an influence upon legal decisions, and so destroy that uniformity which is requisite to the security of individuals. But from these considerations we have nothing to fear upon the present occasion, for the knowledge, integrity and firmness of the bench, will rise superior to every obstacle, and the dignity of their determination will display a lustre awful even to tyranny itself."

The art of the orator to raise the sympathy of his auditors for his cause, and to excite their indignation against these obnoxious acts had undoubtedly a happy effect in propitiating their favor.

" The parties," he continues, "named in the process are of no further consequence than as the one represents the almost forlorn hopes of a disappointed circle; the other as a victim the first destined to the fury of their intemperate zeal and political phrenzy. Why should the abettors of this salutary act as many are pleased to call it, retire behind the curtain on the day of trial, unless something within declares that all is not right? Dare they not appear in the character of informers?—Why

16

should their artillery be leveled against an unfortunate man, who not three weeks since was an object of charity in the streets of Newport, and now a 'poor pensioner on the bounties of an hour,' called upon to answer criminally for refusing beef at four pence the pound, when it cost him six pence on the hoof, although purchased of some of the most influential promoters of the present measures?—Were they dubious of the events, or did they feel a reluctance in attacking gentlemen of business, character and fortune, who daily and openly trample upon their favorite idol?—Were they not acquainted with a Gibbs, and were they not intimately connected with a Cooke?"

"Incomparable was the sentiment of a fine writer, 'that in a democratical government, the customs and manners control the laws,' and whenever an attempt is made to force upon the people a system repugnant to their principles, and at which every sentiment of integrity must reluct, the authors themselves, however sanguine in their hopes, will even betray an instability in the execution that generally forbodes chagrin and disappointment"

Speaking of the act itself, he continues, " the whole frame of it is so replete with blunders, contradictions and absurdities, that not a trace of law learning can be discovered in it. And to the honor of the professional gentlemen, who prefer the good of their country to the paltry gains of business, they had nothing to do with it."

In portraying the effect of *qui-tam* complaints upon public morals, he says, " What is the couse-quence ?—every evil-minded person in the state is invited to turn informer, [a most despicable office,] and more than five hundred prosecutions would take place in the course of a week! Horrid reflec-tion! The idle, profligate and abandoned of every character, would appear in the group of prosecu-tors or witnesses, urged and pushed on by petty conventions and designing juntos, till perjury would run down our streets like a stream, and violence like a mighty river."

After bringing himself before the court and the country, not like a lawyer mechanically discharg-ing a legal obligation to a client, but as the repre-sentative of an oppressed people at an ominous crisis; and fully possessing the favor of the court and audience, he proceeds to lay down his premises. The arguments to enforce them, were then, are now, and ever will be, as sound in doctrine as they are eloquent in expression. For instance, speak-ing of the special trial instituted by this law, un-appealable to, and incontrollable by the Supreme Court, he says, " There are in all free governments three distinct sources of power, the legislative, judiciary and executive. The judiciary power is more or less perfect, as the formation of the courts of law tend to produce a certainty and uniformity in legal determinations. And indeed without certainty and uniformity in judicial tribunals, the best possible system of laws will prove utterly inadequate to the security of the people. For law itself is but a rule of action, and consequently its very existence is destroyed when contrary decisions are admitted upon the same points. From hence may clearly be inferred the necessity of a Supreme Judicial court, to whose judgment, as the only conclusive evidence in law questions, all subordinate jurisdictions must conform."

It is to be regretted, that these sentiments could not have been indelibly imprinted upon the minds of every Rhode-Islander at that day. If they had been, we should not have been destitute of this great egis of protection, until 1833. The solution of the mysterious delay in erecting this necessary attribute of state sovereignty is, that the best offices were worth nothing, and were mere worthless bones for worthless dogs to contend for. It was all party—party—who can most avail us? Has he wealth or connections? How many votes can he bring to the polls? And was he honest—was he capable—was he faithful to the constitution? were requisites not called for.

The argument that it was unconstitutional to make any law, depriving the people of *the trial by jury,* is without exaggeration, one of the most able ever delivered in this country. He proceeds to show the feudal origin of this kind of trial, that it was instituted in England by the Saxons; that it was secured by MAGNA CARTA; that it was the unalienable birthright of every Britain; that the emigrants to America brought it with them. He continues,—"The settlers in this country, from whom we are descended, were Englishmen; they gloried in their rights as such; but being persecuted in matters of religion, over which no earthly tribunal can have the control, they bravely determined to quit their native soil—to bid a final adieu to the alluring charms of their situation, and commit their future existence to that ALMIGHTY POWER, whose authority they dared not to infringe, and in whose protection they could safely confide. They tempted the foaming billows; they braved, they conquered the boisterous Atlantic, and rested in the howling wilderness amidst the horrid caverns of untamed beasts, and the more dangerous haunts of savage men. They retained their virtue, their religion, and their inviolable attachments to the constitutional rights of their country."

" The laws of the realm, being the birthright of all their subjects, followed the pious adventurers

16*

to their new habitations," " and in the charter
granted to this state the same rights are secured
to us, to all intents, constructions, and purposes
whatsoever, as if born in the realm of England.
* * * * The attempts of the British parliament to
deprive us of this mode of trial were among the
principal causes that united the colonies in a defensive war, and finally effected the glorious revolution. This is evident from the declaration of
rights made by the first Congress, the fifth of which
is, ' that the respective colonies are entitled to the
common law of England, and more especially to
the great and inestimable privilege of being tried
by their peers * * * according to the course of
law.' " * * *

"If the first act of the British parliament now
upon record, containing the great charter of the
privileges of the subject—if the exercise of their
privileges for ages—if the first settlement of a new
world to preserve them—if the first solemn compact of the people of this state—if the sacred de-
clarations of the Legislature, at different periods,
and upon the most important occasions—if the solemn appeal to heaven of the United States—in
short, if the torrents of blood that have been shed
in defence of our invaded rights, are proofs? Then
have we triumphed in the cause of humanity—then
have we shown that the trial by jury is the birthright of the people."

Upon the same subject of depriving the citizen

he proceeds, "have the citizens of this state ever
intrusted the legislature with the power of altering
their constitution? If they have, when and where
was the solemn meeting of the people for that purpose? by what public instrument have they declared it, or in what part of their conduct have
they betrayed such extravagance and folly? For
what have we contended, through a long, painful
and bloody war, but to secure inviolate, and transmit unsullied to posterity, the inestimable privileges they received from their forefathers? Will
they suffer the glorious price of their toils to be
wrested from them, and lost forever, by men of
their own creating? They have snatched their liberty from the jaws of the British lion amidst the
thunder of contending nations, and will they base-
ly surrender it to the administration of a year?"

"Constitution have we none:—who dares say
that? None but a British emissary, or a traitor to
his country. Are there any such among us? the
language has been heard, and God forbid that they
should continue!"

"If we have not a constitution, by what authority do our General Assembly convene to make
laws and levy taxes? Their appointment by the

freemen of the towns, excluding the idea of a pre-
existing social compact, cannot separately give
them power to make laws compulsory upon other
towns. They could only meet, in that case, to
form a social compact between the people of the
towns. But they do meet by the appointment of
their respective towns, at such times and places,
and in such numbers as they have been accustomed to do from the beginning. When met they make
laws; consequently they meet, deliberate and en-
act by virtue of a constitution, which if they attempt to destroy, or in any manner whatever infringe, they violate the trust reposed in them, and
so their acts are not to be considered as laws, or
binding on the people."

Commenting on the latter clause of the act,
" without a jury, and according to the laws of the
land," he continues :

" Astounded I am, may it please the honorable
court, that a doubt should have arisen respecting
the construction of our *magna carta*, our declaration of rights. Some of our warmest politicians
whose heads are undoubtedly wrong, and it is
greatly to be feared their hearts are not right, have
boldly asserted that the clause which declares that
no freeman, &c. shall be tried but by the lawful
judgment of his peers, or by the laws of the land,

&c., authorizes any other mode of trial than by jury, should the legislature frame a law for that purpose. That their act would become the law of the land, and so the special jurisdictions are perfectly conformable to the letter and spirit of our constitution."

"Is it possible that these pretenders to the knowledge of the law should be serious, when they avow so dangerous an opinion? If they are, let them be informed, that they contradict the wisdom, and practice of ages—that whenever a statute makes mention of ' the law of the land,' it refers either to a particular pre-existing law, the system of laws in general, or to the mode of legal process."

That the friends of the prosecution were alarmed at the tyrannical stride they had taken, and at the fearful results to the people, is depicted with a keen and indignant reprobation. They began to see their destiny, and Varnum admirably uses it. He said, " well may the countenances of certain gentlemen be changed—well may their trembling limbs denote the perturbation of their minds—well may ' their hearts quake within them.' For all others who, like Empson and Dudley, violate the constitutional laws of their country, deserve, and if they persist in their career, will probably meet their fate."

Other passages from this admirable argument
might be quoted that are cogent and irresistible,
and some others of great beauty, but enough has
been adduced to show the power of the advocate,
and that he has not been eulogized beyond his de-
serts.

In conclusion, when he summed up the cause,
and appealed to the independence and magnanimity of the bench to save their country. When he
represented a powerless Congress and a penniless
nation—the union on the threshold of dissolution,
and the states from sinister and avaricious considerations, shaking off the restraints of the confederation. Demagogues poisoning the minds of an already discontented people—a spirit of misrule stalk-
ing through the land—a political and civil chaos
upheaving the foundations of the republic. When
he showed that Washington and his compatriots
had periled their lives and fortunes in vain—that a
gallant soldiery had endured every suffering, and
shed their best blood for liberty ; that now an independent Judiciary only could save us, and show
to the world, that the experiment of man's capabil-
ity for self government was not a dream, and the
ardent anticipations of the friends of American
liberty had not vanished like the " baseless fabric
of a vision"—and upon them, in the fearless discharge of their duties upon their oaths, the laws

and the constitution, and on them alone, rested the patriot's last hope—that by them we were saved, or by them we perished,—the assembly, by an instantaneous impulse rose from their seats, tears relaxed the stern features of the court, and the countenances of all indicated the overwhelming appeal of the speaker. That the bench and assembly were thus wrought upon is demonstrated by the following conclusion, which nothing but a transported audience and a transported speaker could have warranted or borne.

* * * " Judges, what a godlike pleasure you must feel, having the power, the legal power of stopping this torrent of lawless sway, and securing to the people their inestimable rights. Rest ye venerable shades of our pious ancestors!—our inheritance is yet secure! Be at peace, ye blessed spirits of our valiant countrymen, whose blood hath just streamed at our sides to save a sinking land."

" When the tear is scarcely wiped from the virgin's eye, lamenting an affectionate father, a beloved brother, or a more tender friend!—While the fathers of their country, superior to the ills of slaughter, are completing the mighty fabric of our freedom and independence, shall the decision of a moment rob us of our birthright, and blast forever

our noblest prospects? No! Forbid it, thou Great
Legislator of the Universe! No—

> The stars shall fade away,
> The sun himself grow dim with age,
> And Nature sink in years.
> But thou [fair Liberty] shall flourish in immortal youth,
> Unhurt amidst the war of elements,
> The wreck of matter and the crush of worlds."—*Addison.*

The court adjudged that the amended acts of
the legislature were unconstitutional, and so void.
The fearless independence of the bench overthrew
the tyranny of the demagogues, and the state was
saved. The shops and stores were re-opened, and
the markets which had been illy supplied, were
now amply furnished, and business again assumed
a cheerful aspect. The court were lavishly lauded
by one party, and as severely condemned by the
other. Stung by defeat, the General Assembly
was specially convened by the dominant party on
the succeeding week, by warrant from the Governor. Instant to their object, on the first day of
their session the court were cited to appear before
them, and to show cause for their disloyal judgment, and finally to be dismissed. The comic-
tragic anomaly of one branch of the government
trying the other under the solemn pretext that the
independent decision of the judiciary "tended to
abolish the authority of the legislature."

The General Assembly state on their record,— " Whereas it appears that the honorable Justices of the Supreme Court of Judicature, Court of Assize, &c., at their last September term of said court, in the county of Newport, have, by a judgment of the said court, declared and adjudged an act of the Supreme Legislature of this state to be unconstitutional, and so absolutely void. And whereas, it is suggested that the aforesaid judgment is unprecedented in this state, and may tend to abolish the legislative authority thereof. *It is voted and resolved*, that all the justices of the said court be forthwith cited by the sheriff of the respective counties in which they live, or may be found, to give their immediate attendance on this Assembly, *to assign the reasons and grounds of their aforesaid judgment*. And that the clerk of said court be directed to attend the General Assembly at the same time, with the records of said court, which relate to the said judgment."

They were thus summoned for their trial without the ordinary notice requisite for a legal adjudication by a justice's court, *to assign the reasons and grounds of their judgment* to a co-ordinate branch of the same government. Two of the Judges appeared, the other two were too indisposed to attend. And the General Assembly ordered, " Whereas,

17

from the indisposition of two of the Judges of the Superior Court, this Assembly are prevented from hearing the Justices of the said court, *in respect to the reasons and grounds of their judgment in adjudging an act of this Assembly unconstitutional, and therefore void. Voted and resolved,* that said Justices be cited* to attend this Assembly at their next session, on Thursday of the said session, by the sheriffs of the respective counties, in order to assign the reasons and grounds of their aforesaid judgment."

In order to keep every thing alive, the General Assembly adjourned to the last Monday of the

---

* Copy of the original citation which was served on Mr. Howell.

STATE OF RHODE-ISLAND, &c.

To the Sheriff of the county of Providence, or his Deputy, GREETING.

You are hereby required, in the name of the Governor and company of the said State, to cite David Howell, Esquire, one of the Justices of the said Superior Court, to attend at the General Assembly, to be holden at Providence, on the last Monday of October instant, agreeable to the preceding resolutions, [same as above.] Fail not but make true return hereof. Given under my hand at Providence, the twelfth day of October, A. D. 1786, and in the eleventh year of Independence.

HENRY WARD, *Sec'ry.*

same month, allowing one fortnight for the recovery of the accused, and then to proceed to the trial of

members composing it were sick or well, or however well qualified the exasperated majority might be for impartial triors. At the adjourned session the Chief Justice being still indisposed, could not attend. The three other Judges appeared, " and gave notice, in writing, to both Houses, that they awaited their pleasure." They were informed that the Assembly were ready to hear them, and would proceed immediately upon the business for which they were in attendance.

Certain ceremonies being adjusted, and the records of the court produced, the Hon. David Howell, the youngest Justice, addressed himself to the General Assembly in a very learned, sensible, and elaborate discourse, in which he was upwards of six hours on the floor.

He firstly, pointed out the objectionable parts of the act upon which the information was founded, that it was unconstitutional, and could not be executed.

Secondly—That for the reasons of their judgment upon any question before them, they were accountable to God and their own consciences, and that they were not accountable to the legislature.

Judge Tillinghast observed, that the court accepted their offices with a regard to the public good, that their perquisites were trifling, and their salaries not worth mentioning; that the opinion he had given resulted from the purest reflection, and the clearest conviction. That his conscience testified to the purity of his intentions, and he was happy in the persuasion that his conscience met the approbation of his GOD.

Judge Hazard, who was a paper money man, observed, " that it gave him great pain that the conduct of the court seemed to have met the displeasure of the administration. But their obligations were of too sacred a nature for them to aim at pleasing but in the line of their duty.

" It is well known that my sentiments have fully accorded with the general system of legislation in emiting the paper currency. But I never did, I never will, depart from the character of an honest man to support any measures, however agreeable in themselves. If there could have been a prepossession on my mind, it must have been in favor of the act of the General Assembly; but it is not possible to resist the force of conviction. The opinion," continues this old Roman, "was dictated by the energy of truth. I thought it right—I still think so. Be that as it may, we derived our understand-

countable for our judgment."

To the observations of the judges succeeded a very serious and interesting debate among the members, wherein many arguments and observations were adduced on both sides. At length the question was taken—*Whether the Assembly were satisfied with the reasons given by the Judges in support of their judgment?* It was determined in the negative.

A motion was then made and seconded, "For dismissing the Judges from their offices."

This was coming to the point, for the obtaining of which the greatest exertions had been made. Candidates were upon the spot ready to fill the seats thus made vacant, whom a confidence of success had rendered very importunate.

Upon a question of so unprecedented and so interesting a nature, many of the leading gentlemen of the administration seemed almost ready to yield the ground upon which they had contended,—some were for displacing the Judges at all events; some

17*

were for saving appearances by drawing out a con-
cession on the part of the court, and others were
fully determined to justify them, when the Judges
presented a memorial, which gave a new turn to
the deliberations of the House.

In this memorial, "they stated the facts and
circumstances of their case, and that in the citation to appear before the General Assembly, there
was contained no charge of criminality in their capacity, nor had they reasons to apprehend that any
proceedings were to be grounded thereon to affect
their lives, liberties or property, or their estates in
the office, or their good name or character as officers of this state, and prayed that they might have
a hearing by counsel, before some proper and legal
tribunal, and'an opportunity to answer *certain and
specific charges*, before any sentence or judgment
be passed injurious to their rights and privileges,
and utterly protested against any right in the legislature, by summary vote, to deprive them of their
offices without due process of law; and more especially upon a mere suggestion of a mere error of
judgment."

The memorial being received, the Judges informed the House that they had directed counsel to enforce its contents. Whereupon Gen. Varnum addressed the House in behalf of the Judges, which

speech was copious, argumentative and eloquent. The memorial was enforced upon all its points, and upon the competency and legality of the legislature as triors, he concludes by observing:—

"Let the human heart, and as I have the honor of addressing myself to some who profess, and even attempt to teach the doctrines of Christianity, the conscience also, be consulted on this question! Should not the parties litigant be equally indifferent to the judge, who is to decide upon their controversy? Why is it that jurors may be challenged and removed for favor, but that the mind should be perfectly unbiassed and open to the reception of truth? Why, like Cæsar's wife, should they be incapable of being suspected, unless that the parties themselves might feel a perfect confidence in their judges? Can that confidence be placed on this occasion? Hath not the matter been taken up rather in a political than a judicial point of view? I do not assert, but hath it not been determined, in a convention of part of the members, to remove the judges, and appoint others who will execute, at all events, the penal acts? Hath not one town, in particular, proceeded so far, as to instruct* its depu-

---

* At a town meeting, held at Coventry, in the county of Kent, in the State of Rhode-Island, &c., at the dwelling house of Thomas Waterman, Innholder, on Saturday,

ties to use their utmost influence in bringing the judges to punishment? Is it possible to suppose,

---

the 28th day of October, 1786, called by a warrant from the Town Clerk.

Voted, that the following instructions be, and hereby are, given to William Burlingame and Jeremiah Fenner, who are the representatives for said town for the October sessions of the General Assembly of said state.

First,—that they vote and use their influence in General Assembly that the Judges of the Superior Court of Judicature, &c., be dealt with according to the nature of their offence in giving their determination in the case John Trevett *vs.* John Weeden, in which determination it was thought by the town, that the said Judges exceeded the bounds of their jurisdiction by giving their determination that the law made by the General Assembly of this state was unconstitutional, when it was the duty of said court to have given their judgment whether the said John Weeden was guilty of a breach of the law of this state or not.

Secondly,—we recommend to the said representatives to use their influence in General Assembly, that there be no laws made by this state that will operate against the act for emiting the paper money in May last, so as to weaken and destroy the tender of said money, as is expressed in said act, for if any alteration is made by which the money is not a tender according to said act, we conceive that the bankers will not, nor cannot be justly held to answer the obligations, as the contract made by the state with the bankers must be thereby avoided.

Signed by order,   JOHN RICE, *T. Clerk.*

but that the influence of their constituents will
have some weight in forming their opinion? Can
they be objected to as having prejudged the cause?
If they cannot, is there not a moral certainty of
condemnation? If they can, will not the objection
be so far extended, as to prevent the possibility of
a legal decision."

"Guardians and protectors of the people, seriously reflect upon the magnitude of the present
question, and the important events that may result
from your determination. 'The GREAT JUDGE of
all the earth, can he do wrong?' Of beings rational
he requires the 'heart,' and 'as a man believeth in
his conscience, so is he.' Submit then to the Heav-
enly standard! and as the Judges have acquitted
themselves *conscientiously* in the sight of God and
man, add to the general plaudit, which shall waft
their names upon the wings of immortal fame to
the latest posterity."

"A concise and rational debate followed this
speech in the House, in which the fury of passion,
except in one or two instances, surrendered to cool
reflection, and prepared the way to vindicate the
honor of the law, and the dignity of the state.
Vain was any endeavor to recall the mind to a pre-
determined resolution! Truth exerted her gen-
tle influence, while prejudice and malice retired
abashed."

" A motion was made by an honorable member, seconded and agreed to, that the opinion of the Attorney General, and the sentiments of other professional gentlemen be requested, whether constitutionally and agreeable to law, the General Assembly can suspend or remove from office the Judges of the Supreme Court, without a previous charge and statement of criminality, due process, trial and conviction thereon."

" Mr Channing, the Attorney General, observed, as it was at all times his duty, so he derived a peculiar pleasure in rendering to the honorable Legislature every legal assistance in his power. That he attended the trial upon the information, and was happy in the conviction, that the whole conduct of the Judges demonstrated the greatest candor and uprightness, and according to his private opinion, their determination was conformable to the principles of constitutional law. But be their judgment according to law or not, confident he was, that there would be a fatal interruption, if not an annihilation of government, if they could be suspended or removed from office for mere matters of opinion, without charge of criminality."

Next rose the venerable Dr. Bradford, speaker of the House, and late Lieutenant Governor during the revolutionary war, with whitened locks and patriarchal mein, and paternally addressed them, as a father would address his children. "That he really felt astonished that so much time should be taken up in useless altercations—that he had been honored with a seat in one, or the other, of the Houses of Assembly, for upwards of thirty years, and could not recollect a period in which harmony and unanimity were more essentially wanting than at the present time. That the people of this state had been well governed—that they had been a happy people, and might still be as happy as any on earth, if all party contentions could be laid aside, and every one strove to soothe the cares and heal the wounds of his neighbor. That he besought and entreated the members to embrace the present moment, in which there seemed to be a spirit of conciliation, to put an end to all further contention among themselves, but what might arise for the sake of information! And as they regarded the honor, the peace and the safety of the state, that they would discharge the Judges from any further attendance, and apply themselves in earnest, and with one mind, to such measures as would render them happy at home, and respectable abroad."

Rouse J. Helme, Esq., gave his professional opinion, confirming the positions already taken by those preceding him, and in a lucid exposition of the doctrine of impeachment, and manner of process in trials of this nature.

Mr. Goodwin spoke with elegance, and fully acquiesced in the opinions already given; that no sentence could be passed against the Judges but by regular process, in which the specifications of the charges is essentially requisite. He was diffusely eloquent, enlarged on the subject, and concluded by observing that he had given his sentiments without reserve, and had thought with freedom before he gave them.

The two professional gentlemen, members of the House, the Hon. Mr. Marchant,* and Mr. Bourne,† confirmed the sentiments of their brethren in the leading points. Then the only remaining question was, whether the Judges should be discharged from further attendance upon the General Assembly, as no accusation appeared against them? The question was put and decided by a very large majority.

The record says, " That the three Judges being fully heard before this Assembly, *It is voted and resolved, That no satisfactory reasons have been rendered by them for the judgment on the said in-*

---

* Hon. Henry Marchant, member of the old Congress, and signer of articles of confederation—and afterwards District Judge.

† Hon. Benjamin Bourne, first representative to Congress under the Constitution—District, and then Circuit Judge of the United States Court.

formation, Trevett against Weeden. And that as the Judges of the said Superior Court, &c. are not charged with criminality in giving judgment upon the information, John Trevett *vs.* John Weeden, they are therefore discharged from any further attendance upon this Assembly on that account."

Thus ended one of the most daring and unparalleled usurpations in one part of the government to arraign, try, and adjudicate upon the solemn action and right of the judicial opinion of another department of the same government, while moving in its legitimate sphere, to be found in the records of any civilized state.

But it was eulogium enough on Varnum, that the power of these speeches wrought such a triumphant victory over public opinion, that the dominant party, to save themselves from political prostration, were compelled to repeal their arbitrary and unconstitutional acts, within sixty days from the time of their passage.

The public, having witnessed these forensic efforts of Gen. Varnum, were clamorous for their publication, not doubting but they should feel the same thrilling impressions from their perusal as they had experienced at their delivery. This proved an unfortunate mistake on both sides. The style,

18

manner, and action; the time, place, and circumstances—the *vividus manus, vividi occuli, et omnia
rivida*, of the orator could not appear on paper;—
they had vanished forever.

Their reduction to writing from recollection, after a considerable time had elapsed, after the fire
that had kindled the mighty blaze had gone out,
must have been a vain effort. Candor compels us
to admit, that if the scantling bears but a faint
resemblance to the original, it was worthy of the
great reputation handed down to us by tradition.

General Varnum was not cold and phlegmatic
in his eloquence; his temperament was naturally
ardent, and when excited or aroused by the circumstances or events in his cause, was vehement.—
None can impart warmth, or zeal, that have none
of their own, and to impress an assembly with the
truth or sanctity of our cause, we must ourselves
be convinced that it is true. The secret of Whitefield's overpowering eloquence was, " that he knew,
and tens of thousands felt, that God was with him
of a truth, making the gospel rebound from his
heart to their hearts, melting them by warming
him, winning their souls by absorbing his own with
the glories of salvation." Varnum warmed his
hearers when he spoke, and that warmth would
sometimes give him new fire, and he would some-

times start from his course. When pursuing his subject with an intense zeal, seeing the eyes of the court riveted upon him, and the numerous assembly in extatic emotion, his imagination taking the control, he would fly into a rhapsody. There are such specimens in this speech. They have been used to injure his fame, and it has done so with the critical; but it ought not, when the causes that produced them can be seen as well as felt.

In 1786, Gen. Varnum was again elected a representative to the old Congress, and was an efficient member. At the same session, the distinguished William Samuel Johnson was also a representative from Connecticut. An intimacy was contracted between them, which continued during their lives. This circumstance is mentioned to show why Dr. Johnson spoke of General Varnum, in the case of Smith, of Connecticut, against John Brown, of Providence, in such favorable terms. It was a prize cause of magnitude, and from the parties concerned, and the eminence of the counsel engaged, it excited unusual interest. It was tried before Judge Foster, Judge of the state Admiralty Court at Kingstown. Jesse Root, afterwards Chief Justice of the Supreme Court of Connecticut, and compiler of Root's Reports, opened the case in behalf of Smith, and William Channing, Attorney General of Rhode-Island, and Gen.

Varnum conducted the defence in behalf of Brown, and the distinguished jurist and civilian, Dr. Johnson, of Stratford, closed for the claimant. From the splendor of the talents of counsel, unusual attention was attracted to the scene. The neat, concise, and clear openings by Root and Channing, the brilliant language and thundering eloquence of Varnum, and the calm, placid, unostentatious and classical oratory of Johnson, furnished a legal and intellectual banquet, such as was never seen before, and probably never since in Rhode-Island. To sustain himself againt such power, was victory enough, but Varnum did more, he not only sustained the high expectations of his friends, and the reputation of the Rhode-Island bar, but drove his adversary finally to a nonsuit. Dr. Johnson, whose heart was too magnanimous for envy, besides paying to General Varnum merited compliments in the close, stated at a party, in the evening, " That he knew Gen. Varnum in Congress, and that he was a man of uncommon talents, and of the most brilliant eloquence " We feel assured that Gen. Varnum was justly entitled to this eulogium, or Dr. Johnson would not have given it.

As it is desirable to see the persons, or have presented to you faithful descriptions of distinguished men, a graphic representation of the person, dress, and oratory of Dr. Johnson, has been obtained from the Hon. Asher Robbins, late Senator in Congress, who knew Dr. Johnson well. A sketch of Gen. Varnum has been likewise obtained, and of his manner, dress and appearance, from those who were in daily intimacy with him, that the reader might have both of these great champions before him. Then bring to your mind, in this mental conflict, Dr. Johnson, who Mr. Robbins writes, "in person was the *tout ensemble* of a perfect man, in face, form, and proportion; his stature was above the middle height, say about five feet ten, his eye was dark, and beaming with intelligence, his features regular, and the whole expression of his face, that of benevolence and dignity; his complexion was clear; the hue healthful, not delicate, not robust, but between both; his hair was black with some intermixture of grey, and inclined to curl; his dress of black cut silk velvet. It was the fashion of the bar of that day to be very well, or rather elegantly dressed. I knew of but one exception, that was Ellsworth, afterwards Chief Justice. His dress appeared to be homespun and home made. Dr. Johnson was a highly finished speaker." "I think," continues Mr. Robbins, "that he was the most perfect orator I ever listened to, and I have heard most of the celebrated speakers of my country of my time. In style and manner, if not in matter, he was strikingly superior to them all. In elocution, [in which I include articulation and into-

18*

nation,] he was perfect. And his voice, though so-
norous, was soft, and fell upon the ear like music.
His delivery was deliberate, yet animated; not
slow not rapid, but in a medium between both.
His current and the current of the mind of the
hearer kept pace with each other, and neither out-
stripped the other.   But his great perfection was
his style; his sentences, though apparently prompt
and unpremeditated, were all in the classical cast,
which no meditation could improve, either in the
choice or the collection of the words. Long exercise had made this prompt and classical expression of his ideas habitual to him. His attitude and
motions were full of dignity and grace, and his ges-
tures, though not abundant, were always signifi-
cant."*

* As every incident illustrating the character of Dr.
Johnson will be interesting to the public, the following is
extracted from a recent letter from the Rev. Doctor Jarvis, of Middletown, Connecticut.

"When a child, I was often in his, [Dr. William S.
Johnson's company,] and though he was an old man, the
children gathered round him, as if he was their companion. He was eminently kind to children, and especially
to young persons who showed any fondness for sound
learning. His conversation was always interesting and
instructive. My father, [the late Rt. Rev. Bishop Jarvis,]
told me that when he was in college, [Yale,] a trial occurred of some of the students, at which he, with the

On the other hand appeared Gen. Varnum, with his brick-colored coat, trimmed with gold lace, buckskin small clothes, with gold lace knee bands, silk stockings and boots, [Gen. Barton and himself being the only gentlemen that wore boots all day, at that period,] with a high, delicate and white forehead, with a cowlick on the right side, eyes prominent and of a dark hue, his complexion rather florid. Somewhat corpulent, well propor-

---

other members of the college were present. Dr. Johnson was then, I think, King's Attorney. At all events he was engaged in the trial; and when he spoke, though the court was crowded to suffocation, the attention of the whole assembly was so enchained that, to use my father's expression, ' you might have heard a pin drop.' I have also heard him relate that Dr. Johnson was admitted at college at the age of twelve, and passed a faultless examination in the classics read at that period. But when he was asked for rules of Syntax, his constant answer was, ' Pater meus ita me domit.' I do not know that these anecdotes will be useful to you, but I cannot forbear relating them." * * * * * *

Very respectfully, your obedient servant,

SAMUEL FARMER JARVIS.

" This, [the address to the King by the Congress of 1765,] it is believed was drawn up principally by Mr. Johnson, from Connecticut, one of the ablest lawyers, and most accomplished scholars in America."

Note to Pitkin's Hist. U. S., Vol. I., p. 183.

tioned and finely formed for strength and agility,
large eye brows, nose straight and rather broad,
teeth perfectly white, a profuse head of hair, short
on the forehead, turned up some, and deeply pow-
dered and clubbed. When he took off his cocked
hat he would lightly brush up his hair forward; with
a fascinating smile lighting up his countenance,
he took his seat in court opposite his opponent.
Then imagine the movements, attack, defence and
mental gladiation of these distinguished jurists,
blended with the courtesy of knights, and you have
some tame conception of the reality.

This was the last great effort of Gen. Varnum
in Rhode-Island. At what precise time this trial
took place cannot now be ascertained, as no record
of that court can be found. That it was after the
confederated Congress of 1787, is presumable, because he spoke of their intimacy while in Congress
together. Dr Johnson and Gen. Varnum were not
both members of the same Congress before that
period.

After peace was proclaimed, the General Assembly, taking into consideration the variety of
laws that had been passed, that had originated
from the necessity of the times, and now inapplica-
ble and repugnant to the rights of the people, as
established by the revolution, and it being necessa-

ry to define the distinct powers of the government, and to make provisions for many cases where the laws were silent, resolved that a revision be made of the laws, with such alterations and additions as the circumstances of the state required, and Governor Hopkins, General Varnum and R. J. Helme were appointed the committee for that purpose. It was a work of great labor, requir-

Gen. Varnum was selected by the committee to prepare the digest, and he performed the arduous duty to their satisfaction. Daniel Updike, then a student in his office, transcribed it in a legible hand, for the use of the legislature, and although recommended by another committee appointed to inspect it, the Assembly refused to adopt it, and unfortunately the copy is now lost. It would now be highly interesting to see how the government was arranged, and its several powers defined by a mind like Varnum's.

Thomas Howland, in a communication, states, "that his father was one of the committee to inspect this work, and suggested to Gen. Varnum, [Mr. Howland being a member of the society of Friends,] his objections to the establishment of oaths by law. General Varnum assured him that there was not the name of oath, nor one required to be taken in the whole digest, nor ever to be; if necessary at all, they belonged to the

further observes, " that when the General Assembly sent out the bill, in 1786, to sustain the par value of paper with silver and gold, with a test, or oath, for that purpose, General Varnum addressed the town meeting of East Greenwich;—first, upon the policy of such kind of test, and upon the nature and subject of oaths as they were first introduced; the few and solemn occasions on which they were used, briefly tracing through the Jewish history their multiplication, and the consequent corruption of morals that ensued; very clearly, as well as ingeniously supporting his position from sacred and profane history.   He emphatically closed his remarks by observing, that such was the corruption and degradation to which the people had sank, through the demoralizing effects of oaths at the time of our SAVIOR's appearance, that he left the sacred injunction, "Swear not at all." In these remarks, says *Friend* Howland, "he displayed not only a clearness of vision and power of intellect that fully comprehended his subject, but shone with peculiar brightness.   He was, no doubt, stimulated with the clearest convictions of judgment. In support of the position assumed by Gen. Varnum, I have long considered that a system of civil government altogether distinct and separate from the military code, together with the expulsion of oaths

from our courts of justice, would improve the moral
chara'cter of the community more effectually, and
prot'ect civil rights more securely, than any other
measure that could be adopted."

General Varnúm's attempt to establish a code
of laws for a free state, without the substitute of
affirmations, or some other effective test. in the

the age in which he lived.   By recent enactment,
the British parliament have abrogated oaths from
their Custom house department, but the nation
were not ripe enough in moral progress to carry
the improvement into their courts of justice.

General Varnum was a warm and unwavering
advocate for a federal constitution; he knew the
inefficiency of the confederatio.1; he knew the sel-
fish considerations that governed the states.   If an
instrument cementing the union was not speedily
adopted, he felt that future efforts would be unavailing.   The legal profession, with Gen. Varnum
at their head, the mercantile, and the sound portion of the agricultural interests urged the legislature of Rhode-Island, at their June session, 1787,
in the strongest terms to send delegates to the Federal convention, assembled at Philadelphia.   But
the advocates of the paper money system, and the
revenue accruing to the state from imposts, Rhode-

Island being then the second or 'third importing state, defeated the measure. The minority in the legislature, and those friendly to a Federal constitution, addressed the convention on the subject, and enclosed it to Gen. Varnum to be delivered to that body.*

Congress, by the ordinance of 1787, established the north-western territory. General St. Clair was appointed Governor, September 5th, 1787, and Gen. Varnum and Samuel H. Parsons, Judges in October following. General Varnum left this state to assume his official duties in the spring of 1788, and arrived at Marietta, the established seat of government, in May or June. St. Clair did not arrive until the middle of July, and the Governor and Judges being empowered conjointly to adopt laws for the government of the territory, no duties were performed by the Judges until his arrival.

Marietta was selected by Gen. Rufus Putnam, agent of the New England land company, for a site of a great city. The pilgrim settlers congregated there. It was built at the confluence of the Muskingum with the Ohio, and named after the distinguished but unfortunate Marie Antoinette. It was projected on a magnificent scale. They had their

---

* See Appendix, No. 7.

Campus Martius, sacra via, capitolenum, &c., inscribed upon the plat. But it was an unfortunate location, upon a sterile soil, and it remains to this day an inferior village.

The officers of fort Harmer and Stanwix, the Ohio company, and the citizens intending to celebrate the anniversary of national independence in the new city, the first west of the Ohio, an invitation was tendered to Gen. Varnum, which he accepted, to become their orator. The oration was delivered on the 4th of July, 1788, was published at Newport, in the same year, by order of the directors and agent of the Ohio land company, to which is annexed the speech of Gov. St. Clair, and the proceedings of the inhabitants of this contemplated Queen city of the west.

The oration is short, but contains many beauties both in sentiment and language. It is a rare document, and it is believed that there are not more than two copies now extant, one possessed by the late Mrs. A. C. Greene, a neice of Gen. Varnum's, and the other in Boston. The inhabitants of Marietta have no knowledge of this production, St. Clair's speech, and the other proceedings upon this celebration. An intelligent gentleman of Marietta, and for many years a resident, was surprised that such a work existed, or such an event had occurred; and the fact, incredible as it may seem, is confirmed

19

by Mr. David Putnam, who, by letter, under date of December 7th, 1838, in answer to enquiries respecting Gen. Varnum, observes, "That in the autumn of 1798, I came to this country, forty years ago. With respect to General Varnum, I have nothing to communicate of my own knowledge. He died, as I learn, in February or March, 1789, less than a year after his arrival here. I have enquired of Col. Nye, who arrived here in the autumn of 1788, and has remained here ever since, who states the following,— 'Varnum was a brigadier general in the American revolution, of respectable standing, but not of any distinguished merit; he was bred as a lawyer, and more in repute as a civilian, than a soldier. He came out to the west sometime in the month of May or June, '88, was feeble in health on his arrival, and continued to decline during the fall and winter season, until some time in the month of February or March, 1788. During the winter he was under the management and care of Mrs. Cushing, wife of Col. Nathaniel Cushing, until his death at *Campus Martius*.* The funeral was attended by the military officers of the revolution, Col. Harmer's officers, and an escort from his regiment in military form, and he was buried on the ridge northeast of the mound.† Whether

---

* A stockade built by the first settlers under Putnam.
† "Providence Gazette, March 7, 1789.
On the 10th of January died at Marietta, on the Mus-

there was, or is now, any monument erected at the place, I am not able to say, but am inclined to the belief that stones were erected at the grave. I am not sure, but believe that he was not able to attend at the council of the Indian treaty at fort Harmer, during its progress in November and December, 1788. The government adopted some laws for the

---

kingum, of a lingering disorder, the Hon. Major General James Mitchell Varnum, late of East Greenwich, in this state, one of the Judges of the Supreme Judicial Court in the Western Territory of the United States. A gentleman of very eminent abilities, and not less distinguished for all the social virtues. The public will regret the death of so valuable a citizen—the loss is irreparable to his disconsolate consort. The General's remains were interred at Marrietta with great solemnity and respect. The following was the

ORDER OF PROCESSION.

Marshals.

Mr. Wheaton, bearing the sword and military commission of the deceased on a mourning cushion.

Mr. Mayo, with the diploma and order of the Cincinnati, on a mourning cushion.

Pall Supporters.

GRIFFIN GREENE,

JUDGE TUPPER,

WILLIAM SARGEANT, ESQ.

Marshals.

Mr. Lord, bearing the civil commission on a mourning cushion.

Mr. Fearing, with the insignia of masonry on a mourning cushion.

Pall Supporters.

JUDGE CRARY,

JUDGE PARSONS,

JUDGE PUTNAM.

CORPSE

government of the people of the territory, and made two for the government of the militia. This

Private Mourners.	Private Mourners.
MR. CHARLES GREENE,	MR. RICHARD GREENE,
MR. FREDERIC CRARY,	MR. PHILIP GREENE,
DR. SCOTT,	DR. TINLEY,
DEACON STORY,	DR. DROWN.

PRIVATE CITIZENS.
THIRTY INDIAN CHIEFS.
OFFICERS OF FORT HARMER.
CIVIL OFFICERS.
THE GENTLEMEN OF THE ORDER OF CINCINNATI.
FREEMASONS.

Mr. Clarke, Mr. Stratton, Mr. Leach and Mr. Balch superintended the order of the procession, and the whole were preceeded by Capt Zeigler, of Fort Harmer, with troops and music. A very affecting oration was delivered on the melancholy occasion by Dr. Solomon Drown, of this place, which we hear is to be printed."

CINCINNATI.
Authentic intelligence having arrived of the death of the Hon. General James M. Varnum, Esquire, President of the Society of Cincinnati of the State of Rhode-Island and Providence Plantations, the surviving members of that order in this state, are requested to testify their respect and esteem for the illustrious abilities and virtues of their deceased Brother and President, by wearing the usual signal of mourning upon the *left arm*, twenty-one days, beginning the Sunday following this publication.
ISAAC CENTRE, *Vice President.*
Newport, March 9th, 1789.

is the amount of what I know, says Col. Nye, relating to the person and character of Gen. Varnum.' Mr. Putnam states, "I have never seen his oration, which you say was delivered here July 4th, 1788. He signed ten laws, the last on the 28th November, 1788, which was the last public act of Gen. Varnum. It is not probable that any letters or documents of his are to be found in this country."

It might have been gratifying to his vanity, but Gen. Varnum committed an unfortunate error in accepting the office to which he was appointed. He had impaired his constitution by a free and liberal life, and with an enfeebled physical system, to leave his family, his circle of friends, and the comforts of an old state, and a delightful mansion erected in accordance to his own taste, and ornamented to his fancy, to become a kind of pioneer in a new and unsettled country, among strangers, and in a society uncongenial to his habits, was delusive—fatally delusive. Professional pursuits, in our populous cities, are both more reputable and profitable than any of our national appointments. Yet the overpowering charm of being predistinguished from among the people as capable, or being selected from among our associates as entitled to public honor, is too alluring to individual vanity. But the abandonment of our country, our firesides, and the

19*

endearing connections of home, is a sacrifice too
dear for it all. And so the unfortunate Varnum
found it; on horseback, and attended by a solitary companion, [Griffin Greene,] he left a country that honored him, and an idolizing people, and
traversed eight hundred miles of wilderness, mostly
devoid of the comforts of life. And at his journey's
end was tabernacled in a rude stockade, surrounded by excitements, his disorders aggravated for the
want of retirement and repose, breathing the deadly
exhalations of a great and sluggish river, and pro-
tected, by military array, from the incursions of
the western savage. The issue proved he had no
chance for life, and with a constitution too much
impaired to return, he there lingered and expired.

The following affectionate and interesting letter
addressed to his wife, in the autumn of 1788, announced to her his critical situation, and approaching exit.

" My dearest and most estimable friend,—I now
write you from my sick chamber, and perhaps, it
will be the last letter that you will receive from
me. My lungs are so far affected, that it is impossible for me to recover but by exchange of air and
a warmer climate. I expect to leave this place on
Sunday or Monday next for the falls of the Ohio.
If I feel myself mend by the tour, I shall go no

farther, but if not, and my strength should continue, I expect to proceed to New Orleans, and from thence by the West Indies to Rhode-Island. My physicians, most of them, think the chances of recovery in my favor; however I am neither elevated nor depressed by the force of opinion, but shall meet my fate with humility and fortitude.

"I cannot however but indulge the hope, that I shall again embrace my lovely friend in this world, and that we may glide smoothly down the tide of time for a few years, and enjoy together the more substantial happiness and satisfaction as we have had already the desirable pleasures of life.

" It is now almost nineteen years since Heaven connected us by the tenderest and the most sacred ties, and it is the same length of time that our friendship hath been increased by every rational and endearing motive; it is now stronger than death, and I am firmly persuaded will follow us into an existence of never ending felicity. But my lovely friend the gloomy moment will arrive when we must part; and should it arrive during our present separation, my last and only reluctant thoughts will be employed about my dearest Martha. Life, my dearest friend, is but a bubble, it soon bursts, and is remitted to eternity. When we look back to the earliest recollections of our youthful hours, it seems but the last period of our rest, and we appear to emerge from a night of slumbers to look forward to real existence. When we look forward time appears as indeterminate as eternity, and we have no idea of its termination but by the period of our dissolution. What particular relation it bears to a future state, our general notions of religion cannot point, we feel something constantly active within us, that is evidently beyond the reach of mortality, but whether it is a part of ourselves, or an emanation from the pure source of existence, or reabsorbed when death shall have finished his work, human wisdom cannot determine. Whether the demolition of the body introduces only a change in the manner of our being, or leaves it to progress infinitely, alternatively elevated and depressed according to the propriety of our conduct, or whether we return to the common mass of unthinking matter, philosphy hesitates to decide.

"I know therefore but one source from whence can be derived complete consolation in a dying hour, and that is the Divine system contained in the GOSPEL OF JESUS CHRIST. There, life and immortality are brought to light; there, we are taught our existence is to be eternal. And secure in an interest in the atoning merits of a bleeding SAVIOR, that we shall be inconceiveably happy. A firm and unshaken faith in this doctrine, must raise us above the doubts and fears that hang upon every other system, and enable us to view with a calm serenity the approach of the King of Terrors, and to behold him as a kind and indulgent friend, spending his shafts only to carry us the sooner to our everlasting home. But should there be a more extensive religion beyond the veil, and without the reach of mortal observation, the christian religion is by no means shaken thereby, as it is not opposed to any principle that admits of the perfect benevolence of deity. My only doubt is, whether the punishment threatened in the *New Testament* is annexed to a state of unbelief which may be removed hereafter, and so restoration take place, or whether the state of the mind at death irretrievably fixes its doom forever. I hope and pray that the divine spirit will give me such assurances of an acceptance with God, through the merits and sufferings of his Son, as to brighten the way to immediate happiness.

" Dry up your tears, my charming mourner, nor suffer this letter to give too much inquietude. Consider the facts at present as in theory, but the sentiments such as will apply whenever the change shall come.

" I know that humanity must and will be indulged in its keenest griefs, but there is no advantage

in too deeply anticipating our inevitable sorrows.
If I did not persuade myself that you would conduct with becoming prudence and fortitude, upon
this occasion, my own unhappiness would be greatly increased, and perhaps my disorder too, but I
have so much confidence in your discretion as to
unbosom my inmost soul.

"You must not expect to hear from me again
until the coming spring, as the river will soon be
shut up with ice, and there will be no communication from below, and if in a situation for the purpose I will return as soon as practicable.

"Give my sincerest love to all those you hold
dear. I hope to see them again, and love them
more than ever. Adieu, my dearest friend. And
while I fervently devote in one undivided prayer,
our immortal souls to the care, forgiveness, mercy
and all prevailing grace of Heaven in time and
through eternity, I must bid you a long, long, long
farewell.

JAMES M. VARNUM.

However afflictive must have been this intelligence to his solitary consort, it was alleviated by the
consoling conviction that the benign influence of
the gospel had softened and smoothed the pillow
of death, and shed its acceptance and grace upon

him. That he died a devoted Christian none have reason to doubt.

The career of Gen. Varnum was active but brief. He graduated at *twenty*—was admitted to the bar at *twenty-two*—entered the army at *twenty-seven*—resigned his commission at *thirty-one*—was member of Congress the same year—resumed his practice at *thirty-three*—continued his practice *four* years—was elected to Congress again at *thirty-seven*—emigrated to the west at *thirty-nine*, and died at the early age of *forty*. From the time of his admission to the bar to his departure from the state, was *seventeen* years—deducting the *four* years he was in the military service, and *three* years he was in Congress, his actual professional life was only *ten* years.

Those who are impressed with the opinion that Gen. Varnum was not well read and studious, are wrongfully so. He was periodically an intense student, and would be secluded for weeks. He possessed the rare power of great mental abstraction, and philosophic ratiocination. He was master of his cases, and all the facts were well arranged and digested for trial. Varnum told a friend that he studied his cases in bed, and often had his books brought to him. This is the solution of the myste-

ry which some thought was intuition, of instantly
rising in court and arguing his cause to public surprise and admiration, without any apparent previous preparation or consultation.   He was a great
admirer of Vattel and Montesqueiu, the latter he
would almost repeat.   He delighted in, and cultivated his taste for the poets.   Shakspeare, Young,
Pope and Addison, he would recite with great
readiness, and when a novel came into his hands,
his meals were suspended until it was finished.

Early in life General Varnum married Martha,
the eldest daughter of Cromel Child, of Warren,
in Rhode-Island, a family of very considerable distinction.   Mrs. Varnum was an amiable, virtuous
and high minded lady, and one of the most cheerful, sociable and best of wives.   She survived her
husband forty-eight years, and died at Bristol,
without issue, October 10th, 1837, at the advanced
age of eighty-eight years.

General Varnum was represented to be a kind
and affectionate husband, a steady and useful
friend, highly esteemed and respected by his professional brethren, and a gentlemen of courteous
manners.

STANZAS,

IN MEMORY OF THE LATE HON. JAMES M. VARNUM, ESQ., ONE OF
THE JUDGES FOR THE WESTERN TERRITORY.

STERN king of terrors! sòv'reign of the grave
Arm'd with the two-edged scythe, and ever sounding bow,
Whose pale-fac'd courser dares to meet the brave,
Tread down imperial chiefs, and lay whole myriads low—
One word—no more—draw back thy out-stretch'd hand,
Nor point the mortal shaft at *Varnum's* guileless breast:
Avaunt—begone—from *Marrietta's* land,
And pour thy wrath on *Ouaitanon's* scalp-plum'd crest."

Thus thousands spake.—Death poiz'd his dart in air—
A moment paus'd—and then indignantly reply'd,
" To northern gales I give your ardent prayer,
And all my bosom swells with rage—revenge—and pride:
Shall *Varnum* live, to bind in concord's chain
Fierce mad'ning cannibals beyond *Missouri's* flood?
Tame the grim Sachem of *Ontario's* plain,
And dash from *Analgonquin's* lips the shell of blood?

"Curst be the power that thus disputes my sway,
Bids the wild biped melt at agony's loud groan,
Turns back *Areskoui* chacing man for prey,
And seats Humanity on *Hunda's* flame-girt throne:
Avaunt—begone—Compassion—Pity fly—
Not Empire's unioned force shall blunt the levell'd dart—
Varnum must fall—or Death is doom'd to die!"
He ceas'd—twang'd Fate's shrill bow—and pierc'd him to the
  heart.   G.

[*Massachusetts Magazine.*

In conclusion, it may with propriety be observed,
that the biography of General Varnum is a work
too onerous and responsible for an ordinary hand.

The attempt was burthened with fearful apprehensions. The subject is surrounded by so many embarrassing circumstances, that the hope to fulfil public expectation, or satisfy the anxiety of friends, cannot be anticipated. To delineate the lights and shades of his short but brilliant career, needs a graphic pen, a philosophic mind, and a nice, discriminating taste. And to a reflecting mind, the question presents itself, whether his character and fame would not go down to posterity brighter and stronger from tradition, through the recollections of his friends and cotemporaries, than by the hands of the most skilful biographer?—It is not every character, however distinguished in its day, that has been preserved in biography. The celebrated Patrick Henry has been injured, although his character was drawn by the hand of Wirt. The magic powers of the great Whitefield, the secret of his overwhelming eloquence, and the cause of his influence over the passions of congregated thousands, are not to be found in his published works. His sermons draughted by himself are contemptible compared with his fame; and his printed volumes derogate from his high reputation. His virtues, his talents and his oratory, would have gone down to posterity with far greater eclat, if he had never left a printed line. The historian, Hume, has done more to impress upon posterity Whitefield's vast and enrapturing power, by repeating the following apostrophe, than he ever did for himself. He heard him and observes, that after a solemn pause, he thus addressed his audience,—" The attendant angel is just about to leave the threshold and ascend to Heaven, and shall he ascend and not bear with him the news of one sinner among this multitude reclaimed from the error of his ways." He stamped, lifted up his hands and gushing eyes to Heaven, cried aloud;—" Stop, Gabriel! stop!—ere you enter the sacred portals, and carry with you the news of one sinner converted to God."

Chesterfield heard him on the parable of the prodigal son, and where he represented him tottering and reeling on the precipice of destruction, now recovering, now falling, at last ejaculated that he was lost. The congregation exclaimed out in terror as if at the disastrous reality. These two distinguished scholars, and Cowper and Franklin, have done more to immortalize Whitefield in his own day, and with posterity, than all his biographers together, and but for them his transcendant reputation would have come down to us as the empty impulses of a ranting enthusiast.

And would it not have been better for the character and reputation of Varnum, if he had never left a printed line?—That he was an orator, in all the majesty, sublimity and subduing force of the art, from cotemporary evidence, no one can doubt. That his eloquence would captivate courts and juries, and overwhelm assemblies, none, for a moment, can hesitate to believe. And would it not be safer for his friends, and more for his own character and glory, that his memory should go down to posterity from the traditionary recollection of those who witnessed his great oratorical skill and efforts, than to gather his biography from the memorials left behind him.

That Gen. Varnum was a fine scholar,—that he was a profound lawyer,—that he was an accomplished gentleman, and that he was as brilliant an orator as the age or country produced, are facts established by testimony that does not leave the trace of a doubt. It is enough to mention that the great Stratford Johnson and Thomas Paine* have borne decisive testimonies of his fame, besides a host of cotemporaries, living and dead, confirmatory of them. This unanimity of opinion dissipates all cavil, and candor requires posterity to admit that, that reputation was then, as now, no more than what was justly, honestly and rightfully due to this distinguished man, and adds another bright illustration to the aphorism, " *orator non fit.*"

If, in this imperfect memoir, any thing has been

---

* See the Letter from the Hon. N. F. Dixon, Senator in Congress—Appendix No. 8.

said, that shall in any wise detract from the well-
earned reputation of Gen. Varnum, pardon is un-
feignedly asked of his ashes. If a single remaining friend shall be offended, it will be sincerely la-
mented. To do any thing unjust, or to utter one
sentiment that will diminish from his virtues, his
talents or his fame does *not* belong to one who has
ever been his ardent and enthusiastic admirer.
From what researches have been made, it conscientiously can be stated that, " he was a man of
boundless zeal, of warm feelings, of great honesty,
of singular disinterestedness ; and, as to talents, of
prodigal imagination, a dexterous reasoner, and a
splendid orator. * * * * He was a man made upon
a gigantic scale ; his very defects were masculine
and powerful. He reminds us of one of those stern
figures which cross the eye in the landscapes of
Salvator Rosa, extravagantly spirited, and wildly
great. * * * He is gone, however, to a tribunal
where, perhaps, the excesses of *life* are less severely
punished than its deficiencies ; and the delinquen-
ces of the head less visited than those of the heart.
While he lived, the obtrusiveness of his faults
might have inclined us to a judgment dispropor-
tionably harsh. But now that he is brought before
us, like the kings of Egypt, for judgment, we must
take care to administer deliberate justice, without
forgetting the claims of CHARITY."

20*

MATTHEW ROBINSON,

Was the only son of Robert Robinson, who was appointed searcher of the Customs in Newport, by Queen Anne, and assumed the duties of the office about the year 1706. Mr. Robert Robinson also had a daughter who was, in early life, bereft of her reason, and who survived him. He removed to Narragansett, and resided with his son some time before his death, and was buried on the farm where his son resided. Handsome tombstones were erected to his memory, which are now standing, with the following inscription:

HERE LIES THE BODY OF

ROBERT ROBINSON, Esquire,

Late Searcher of his Majesty's Customs for this Colony. Who sustained many honorable posts under the reigns of Queen Anne, King George 1st and King George 2d. He departed this life in the ·

84TH YEAR OF HIS AGE, JAN. 8TH, A. D. 1761.

Matthew was born in Newport, in the year 1709. He was well educated, and was an apt and ready Latin and Greek scholar, but whether he graduated from any public institution cannot now be ascertained. He studied law in Boston, and established an office in Newport, about forty years before the rĕvolution. He married Mrs. Johnson, the mother of Augustus Johnson, [afterwards Attorney General,] who was the daughter of Mr. Lucas, a French Huguenot, of some wealth and distinction, who had fled from his country upon the revocation of the edict of Nantz.* Mr. Robinson practised law at Newport with reputation, and his business was considerable on the circuits. He moved to Narragansett about the year 1750. The particular motives for this change of residence are unknown. He bought fifty acres of land in his first purchase, to which he subsequently made large additions, so that his whole estate finally contained about eight hundred acres, which he continued to improve during his life. He erected upon it a mansion house after the style of the English lodge, which displayed great taste for appearance and convenience. He called it Hopewell. It is now standing, about one hundred rods from the Kingston depot, in a state of dilapidation. His wife, the daughter of Mr. Lucas, died soon after his removal to Narragan-

---

* Upon Mr. Lucas's arrival at Newport, he hired an estate of Mr. Robert Gardner, for his residence. He brought with him a graft of the celebrated *Gardner Pear,* and reared it in his garden. About the time the tree began to bear, Mr. Gardner occupied his own estate, and the pear remaining, it obtained the name of the Gardner, instead of the Lucas Pear. I have made this note for the benefit of the Pomologist.

sett. She was highly esteemed as an exemplary and accomplished lady, and her death was an afflictive dispensation to her husband. From the severity of this bereavement he never recovered. His circumstances, from this event, finally became disarranged through professional absence, improvident overseers, and negligent domestics.

Mr. Robinson was a well read and learned man, and deeply and critically so in the old and intricate doctrine of estates, and Coke upon Littleton, was his favorite work. His library was large, and well selected in law, history, and poetry; probably the largest possessed by any individual in this state at that day; among which were many French authors, that came into his possession through his father-in-law. Mr. Lucas' Huguenot Bible, an elegant folio edition, is now in the neighborhood in a good state of preservation. He possessed a rare and valuable collection of pamphlets, magazines and ephemeral productions of the times, and was industrious in the collection and preservation of all the interesting works of the day, endorsing his own remarks upon them; and if anonymous, who were the reputed authors; what was his own and public opinion upon their merits. He was scrupulously reluctlant to loan them, and if he did, it was duly entered in his book. Taking all his works together, those that were purchased, and those that were presented to him, what he carefully noted on them, no doubt exists that he possessed, before his death, a more curious and valuable collection for antiquarian information than any other person in the state, if not in New England. Whatever rare productions have been, or now are extant in the Narragansett country, mostly came from his library. He was a great antiquarian himself, and embraced, in his character, the elements of great curiosity, inquisitiveness and research. He prided himself on his critical knowledge of English history, and every circumstance relative to the settlement of America, and particularly of Rhode-Island, and all the families and estates in it.

Mr. Robinson was a great student to the latest period of his life, and read aloud daily, as long as his health would permit. He was, withal, a singular and pedantic genius, with great information, but mostly derived from books, without any great knowledge of human nature. He had treasured up a great mass of queer and comparatively useless knowledge, unserviceable for human life.— There are many anecdotes of him extant, which, when divested of manner, are too lifeless to repeat. He was a great collector of amazing incidents, trite sayings and conundrums, which he preserved in a book kept for that purpose. One was, " that it was difficult to drive a black hog in the dark."

He kept a journal of the events of the day, with his remarks upon them. For instance, " J. Stauton has been to my house this day, and told a story an hour long, the amount of it was, that Col. Potter had said that by the law that the General Assembly had passed, paper money would be equal to gold, all which I believe to be a *lie.*" And others singular and entertaining. This journal was in existence in 1806, and great merriment would be excited upon its perusal. But upon the severest inquiry it cannot now be found. It has, probably, like a vast many other curious and priceless productions, been used to light fires, or test the temperature of curling tongs.

Mr. Robinson enjoyed a great share of practice, and was generally engaged in all the causes in the courts. But I cannot learn that there were, at that period, any cases of great magnitude or interest, and probably there were not any very exciting ones during his practice. His services were highly useful as one of the committee, of which he was chairman, for investigating the disputed claim between this colony and Massachusetts, respecting the still unsettled controversy of the northern boundary. Some of his reports are found to be very serviceable to the present counsel employed upon that trial. He was chairman of the committee to draw up a history of the whole case, by order of the Legislature, for the use of Henry Marchant, Esq., then Attorney General, who was appointed special agent to England, in 1771, with their resident agent, Mr. Sherwood, with instructions to lay the same before the King in Council, and obtain, through commissioners, an adjustment of that irritating subject.

Mr. Robinson was opposed to the revolution in principle, but was neutral in action. He felt himself conscientiously bound by the oath of allegiance, and questioned the sufficiency and validity of the causes for separation. He had lived quietly under the government for seventy years. Its glory was his glory. He feared we were not ripe for the hazardous change. He doubted the success of the experiment. He abhorred an alliance with our old enemy, the French. He dreaded that a steady government might be succeeded by anarchy. His constitution was nervous, his disposition irritable, and naturally impatient of contradiction. He had been provoked into some hasty, imprudent and sarcastic remarks upon the character of the contest, which coming to the knowledge of the Legislature, in January, 1781, the following resolution was adopted. "Whereas the Assembly hath received information, that Matthew Robinson, Esq., of South Kingstown, hath, in his conduct and conversation publickly manifested principles inimical and dangerous to the liberties of the Uni-

ted States of America, *Resolved*, that the said
Matthew Robinson be taken into custody by the
sheriff of King's county, and committed to the jail
in said county, and be there confined until further
order of this Assembly."

The incarceration of Mr. Robinson created a
deep sympathy in all who were acquainted with
him.   Mr. Henry Marchant, one of the leaders of
the revolutionary party in. this state, who lived
near him, and others, ardent and active friends of
the American cause, knowing the natural irrita-
bility of his temper, his age and infirmity of constitution, that he might easily be betrayed into indis-
cretions, though in general of a peaceful demeanor,
took a warm interest for his liberation.   Through
their recommendations, Gov. Cooke, to whom Mr.
Robinson was also well known, prompted by the
humanity of his character, ordered his discharge
upon his own responsibility upon Mr. Robinson's
parole to restrain himself within his own house.

The General Assembly, in February, approved
of the benevolence of this act of the Governor,
and " *Voted*, that his Excellency, the Governor, in
removing Matthew Robinson from the jail, in Kings
county, and confining him to his own house, considering the condition of said jail, and the said Robinson's state of health, be, and the same is hereby

approved, he having the liberty of his farm, and not going without the bounds thereof until the further order of the Assembly." In March, Mr. Robinson appeared before them, and made an exposition, which was satisfactory; and the Assembly *resolved*, that he be discharged from his said confinement, and that he be restored to all the rights and liberties he before enjoyed, and that he appear before the next Assembly, if required," and thus the matter ended.

The preceding incident exhibits a bright example of the political tolerance and patriotic magninimity of the revolutionary leaders, and the high respect the members of the legal profession entertained for an aged brother in promptly liberating from confinement a feeble, irritable, but good hearted old man. For the exertions of his friends upon this critical occasion, Mr. Robinson, to the latest period of his life, expressed the deepest gratitude.

In the latter part of his life Mr. Robinson became so infirm that he was employed but occasionally, and probably this infirmity was hastened by his imprudently becoming surety for his step son, Augustus Johnson, who dying insolvent, greatly embarrassed Mr. Robinson in his pecuniary circumstances, and perplexed his latter days. It was

in defence of one of these suits, instituted against
him, as Johnson's surety, in the Circuit Court of
the United States, before Judge Jay, at Newport,
that Mr. Robinson made his last forensic effort.
Out of respect to his age, his long and respectable
standing at the bar, and his great respectability as
an octogenarian advocate, the Judge permitted
him unchecked, to take his own course and to occupy as wide a range of discussion as his fancy
could desire. The good, and ever to be respected
Judge, after his return to New York, wrote to Mr.
Robinson, complimenting him on his superannuated
efforts. This very flattering letter to the most aged
lawyer in practice on the circuits, was carefully
preserved by him during life; but it is to be regretted that it is now lost.

Mr. Robinson's house was the mansion of hospitality,—he was fond of good society, and entertained much company, and the well informed and
learned were welcome guests. Dr. MacSparran,
the Rev. Mr. Honyman, Fairweather and Besset,
Daniel Updike, James Honyman, John Aplin, Joseph Aplin, Judge Lightfoot, Dr. Moffatt, John
Cole, Judge Marchant, and William Ellery, were
his frequent and intimate friends and were always
cordially received.

Out of respect to the memory and regard for the
reputation of this singular and learned man, many

like now to visit Hopewell, the place of his residence, and the frequent resort of his distinguished
guests, and indulge an hour of solemn retrospec-
tion on the *bye gone* days of Mr. Robinson, and reflect, that under that dilapidated roof, and at his
social board, once a learned host of his intellectual
associates were often collected, all of whom have
gone to the dust.

At the request of Mr. Benjamin Hazard, of Newport, who had seen Mr. Robinson, and heard his
last effort at the bar, and who for his age and talents entertained a high respect, an afternoon stroll
was taken to this consecrated spot, and a walk over
its grounds. An aged neighbor* present, who had
known Mr. Robinson many years before his death,
pointed out to us the stone below the curve in the
limpid stream, near his house, into which he would
throw his line, enjoying the delightful retrospec-
tion, that the venerable Canonicus, the unfortunate
Mantinomah, and the brave Canonchet, the last of
the Naragansetts had, standing on the same stone,
drawn out the golden trout before him. Then,
there were his rows of box, here his beautiful tall
sycamores, there his spacious garden, arranged
with exotic plants, and on this extended green was
his morning and evening walk. And when we en-

---

* Mr. Robert Brown.

tered Hopewell lodge, this was his library, this his dining room, and there stood his arm chair; and this the recess where he kept his books for daily use; this the drawn shelf on which he wrote, and here the place where stood his box of snuff; this the room in which he slept, and where he died. My companion seated himself in his arm chair, overcome by the hallowed reminiscences of the past, and in a *Swedenborgian reverie*, corresponded with the spirits of the departed.

Mr. Robinson, in July, 1795, made his will, and most humanely provided for his unfortunate sister, who had continued through life under the distressing bereavement of reason. She survived her brother but a few weeks. In October of the same year, Mr. Robinson died at his mansion, in South Kingstown, insolvent, at the advanced age of eighty-six years. His estate, including his family pictures,* books, pamphlets and papers, were sold at auction; and it is said, with a blush, that a lawyer was the executor, and his valuable library was put up and sold by the single volume, without regard to sets or editions, and were irretrievably scattered.

---

* The portraits of his father and mother were purchased by the late Hon. Elisha R. Potter, and are now remaining in the mansion of his son, at Kingston.

Mr. Robinson, in stature, was about five feet six inches in height, very spare in person, a mere shadow, with a bright, piercing black eye. His voice was shrill and sharp, and his manners courteous, except when excited. He was interred in the family burial ground on his farm; a large concourse of people attended his funeral in testimony of their respect for his talents and character, but it is lamentable to reflect that there are no stones. with any inscription, standing at his grave.

21*

ROBERT LIGHTFOOT.

ROBERT LIGHTFOOT was born in London, in 1716. His family were wealthy, and of high respectability. He graduated from the University of Oxford, studied law in the Inner Temple, and was appointed Judge of Vice Admiralty, in the southern district of the United States, in the reign of George II., with a salary of £600 a year. He entered upon the duties of his office, but the climate enfeebling his health, he came to Newport, which was then, as now, celebrated for its restorative influence, to renovate his impaired constitution. Finding the island and its scenery as delightful as his fancy could sketch, and its society refined and attractive, he was disinclined to return, and resigned his office.

Judge Lightfoot was an accomplished classical scholar, and his intellectual acquirements were extensive. His general deportment was grave, but he was a great wit and humorist, when he chose to be. His society was courted by every social and literary circle. The venerable Dr. Waterhouse, in his letter, observes·* "I knew Judge Lightfoot very well; he was a Judge of Admiralty, a very

* See Appendix, No. 6 and 7.

well educated, idle man. I knew his sisters in Lon-London, single and opulent. He first taught me to value and study Lord Bacon, and from him I learnt to value Locke and Newton and Bœrhaave. He was the oracle of literary men in Newport. After more than seven years absence in Europe, he called upon me in the town of Cambridge. He was a very able and learned man, and was, at Rhode-Island, I thought,

> * * * * 'condemned to trudge
> Without an equal, and without a judge.'

He was a great epicure, a perfect encyclopedia, and welcome to every table of the first characters, and constantly dined from home. He was not a buffoon or mimic, but a fine relator of apt anecdotes. He informed every body, and contradicted no one, but had a happy Socratic method of teaching. He honored me with his notice, and I gained more knowledge from him than any other man in the choice of books. I am not certain that he ever read law as a profession, yet he was master of it as well as of the science of medicine. And in our highest paroxisms of party politics, he had the rare art of veiling his contempt. Next to Dr. Fothergill, I owe Judge Lightfoot more than any other man I can name. He taught me to strip off the husk from the *cocoa-nut* of learning so as to come at the meat. During thirty years that I gave lectures in the University of Cambridge, I endeavored to display the pages of Locke, Bacon and Linnæus,

but I should hardly have been able to have done
what little I have, had I never known Lightfoot."

The above extract is but a just eulogium on
Lightfoot; he was all that the venerable Doctor
has described. The people of Newport talk of
their city as it was before the revolution, in the
palmy and classical days of Lightfoot, and mourn
over those departed times when their island was the
intellectual constellation of this western hemis-
phere. She was ornamented with her Hunter, her
Haliburton and Moffat, in medicine and surgery.
Brown, Clapp, Callender, Honyman, Styles, Hopkins and Thurston, in the ministry, and for a while
illumined by the residence of Berkely—and Lightfoot, Updike, Scott, Robinson, Ellery, Johnson,
Honyman, Marchant, Channing, Simpson, and
others, within her bar. And her general society,
learned, polished and urbane. To which was added erudite and accomplished strangers, military
and naval, induced from the love of science and
the charm of climate to resort there. Truly and
emphatically may she lament the disastrous change,
and weep over the classical reminiscences of her
departed splendor.

The sisters spoken of by Dr. Waterhouse, char-
acteristic of opulence, kept their chariot in London. They ever expressed a feeling attachment
for their brother. They informed him that by kin-
ship he was entitled to a thousand pound sterling,

which was deposited in the Bank of England for

be advanced, if his necessities required it. Frances
Lightfoot was his daughter. She was well instructed by her father, and was an amiable, sensible lady. She survived him many years, and died
at William Robinson's, in Newport, in whose family, after the death of her father, she became a
resident. His sisters, in London, having been informed that their brother had a daughter, wrote
him that if he would furnish the necessary evidence
of the existence of a legitimate child, she should
be the heir to their fortunes.

The time and manner of relating his anecdotes,
the appearance of the man, the turn of the eye and
change of countenance were in such keeping with
the incidents related, that they were inimitable, and
would keep the coterie in a constant glee, but when
repeated by others are insipid.

The ordinary repasts, with Lightfoot, are remembered; during his visits other gentlemen would be
congregated. After *dining*, a few glasses of wine
were customary; and then followed "the feast of
reason and the flow of soul." Disquisitions on various subjects, historic incidents and lively anecdotes; and after the company had withdrawn from
table, Hudibras was occasionally introduced, and
Lightfoot read in his inimitable style, and dis-

coursed upon the times and characters delineated in it. Dr. Rush relates, that when in Edinburgh, he heard Milton read by a gentleman in a style and emphasis so beautiful and new to him, that he should not have known it to have been the same work. In a similar manner Lightfoot read Butler's Hudibras.

The Judge abhorred pedantry. One of the Appleton's vainly priding himself in classical attainments, to his great annoyance was in the habit of throwing out quotations from Homer and Hesoid. The Judge becoming vexed beyond further endurance, asked him if he recollected this line,

Shoulderoi moiton kia pasteroi venison.

Appleton replied, he well recollected that beautiful line of Hesoid, and the Judge was well satisfied with the quiz.

He was an apt relater of anecdotes; he told an incident of one of his journies to Connecticut. He stated, he once travelled from Newport to Pomfret, and was overtaken by a snow storm without an overcoat. He stopped at a public house for refreshment, and the inquisitive landlady propounded to him several questions. Where he was from? from Newport;—where was he bound? to visit the six nations;—had he no great coat? he never wore one; how many children he had? nine. She screamed out, husband, husband;—come here;—

here is a man with nine children, and never wears
a great coat, when I have made you a dozen, and
we never had one!'

The time of Judge Lightfoot was spent in reading and visiting. His routine was from Newport
to Narragansett, and from thence to Godfrey Mal-
bones, in Pomfret, Connecticut. He occasionally
visited Mr. Auchmuty and Attorney General Gridley, his intimate friends, and others, at Boston.
The literary men extended to him their hospitali-
ties wherever he was known. Previous to his
death, he took up his residence at Plainfield, in
Connecticut. The late Hon. Calvin Goddard, in
a communication, observes, "That in Brooklyn
there is an Episcopal Church, and in the grave
yard contiguous are deposited the remains of
Judge Lightfoot. He died suddenly at Plainfield,
in 1794, soon after I commenced the practice of
the law there. I remember him well, but I was
young, and he was old, and was not very intimate
with him. He was supported, as I understood, and
for many years had been, by two or three maiden
sisters, in England; by whom, it is said, his drafts
for that purpose were always honored. His family
consisted of himself and his daughter Fanny; they
had a small comfortable house, and lived retired.
The daughter was a well informed young lady, and
much respected. I remember one peculiarity about
him, which was standing in the street, or elsewhere,

with the little finger of one hand apparently scratch-
ing a particular spot on his head, and when his head
was uncovered, there was a spot on it made bare by
that operation. This, among common observers,
was evidence of great thoughtfulness, or absence
of mind. He had a library, but not very large,
but probably read considerably. I recollect of
seeing at his house, among other works, an entire
set of the journals of the House of Commons up
to some short period prior to the revolution. There
was not much literary society in Plainfield. Dr.
Benedict had more learning than most country
clergymen. The Rev. Mr. Fogg, the Episcopal
clergyman, at Brooklyn, was quite respectable in
that respect, and Judge Lightfoot, when he attended worship any where, went there. On his grave
stone is this inscription.

SACRED

TO THE MEMORY OF

JUDGE ROBERT LIGHTFOOT.

He was born in England, educated at Oxford.

DIED AT PLAINFIELD,

AGED ABOUT 78 YEARS

The stone says about seventy-eight years, that
is all I presume is known, for I remember it was
said, that nothing made him more angry than any
enquiries about his age."

APPENDIX.

No. I.—[p. 34.]

ROGER WILLIAMS' TESTIMONY IN FAVOR OF RICHARD SMITH'S TITLE TO THE WICKFORD LANDS

Nahiggonsett, [Narragansett] 24 July, 1679. [ut vulgo.]

I, ROGER WILLIAMS, of Providence, in the Nahiggonsett bay, in New England, being, [by God's mercy,] the first beginner of the mother town of Providence, and of the colony of Rhode-Island and Providence Plantations, being now nearly four score years of age; yet, [by God's mercy,] of sound understanding and memory; do humbly and faithfully declare, that Mr. Richard Smith, sen., who for his conscience to God left fair possessions in Glostershire and adventured with his relations and estate to New England, was a most acceptable inhabitant, and prime leading man in Taunton, in Plymouth colony. For his conscience sake, [many differences arising,] he left Taunton and came to the Narragansett country, where by God's mercy, and the favor of the Narragansett Sachems, he broke the ice [at his great charge and hazard] and put up in the thickest of the barbarians the first English house among them.

22

2. I humbly testify that about forty years ago from this date, he kept possession, coming and going himself, children and servants, and he had quiet possession of his houses, lands and meadows, and there in his own house, with much serenity of soul and comfort, he yielded up his spirit to God, the father of spirits, in peace.

3. I do humbly and faithfully testify as aforesaid, that since his departure his honored son, Capt. Richard Smith, hath kept possession, [with much acceptation with English and Pagans,] of his father's houses, lands and meadows, with great improvement, also by his great cost and industry, and in the late bloody Pagan war, I knowingly testify and declare, that it pleased the Most High to make use of himself in person, his houses, his goods, corn, provisions and cattle, for a garrison and supply to the whole army of New England, under the command of the ever to be honored Gen. Winslow, in the service of his Majesty's honor and country of New England.

4. I do also humbly declare, that the said Richard Smith, Jun., ought by all the rules of equity, justice and gratitude to his honored father and himself, to be fairly treated with, considered, recruited, honored, and by his Majesty's authority confirmed and established in a peaceful possession of his Father's and his own possessions in this Pagan wilderness and Narragansett country.

The premises I humbly testify, as now leaving the country and this world

ROGER WILLIAMS.

1641. Richard Smith purchased a tract of the Narragansett sachems, among the thickest of the Indians, [computed 30,000 acres] erected a house for trade, and gave free entertainment to travellers; it being the great road of the country.   [Mass. Hist. Coll. vol. i. p. 216.

The house of Smith stood on the site of the present Updike house, in North Kingstown, and it is said the present house contains some of the materials of the ancient one; bricks [in the front ten feet high, are the same as were the old front of the fort.]   The very first house built by Smith was probably a block house.

The great road for all the travel from Boston, and the north and east, to Connecticut and New York, passed by this house, following the course of the shore, probably very near the route of the present post road through Tower Hill, Wakefield, Charlestown and Westerly.   It was a very ancient path, and is often referred to in the old deeds, &c., as a "country road,"—the "road to Pequot,"—the "Pequot Path."

Within a few years after this, trading houses were built in Narragansett by Roger Williams and Wilcox.   Roger built within seven or eight years after Smith, and not far from him, [Williams' trading house was where Royal Vaughan last lived, the next house north of Spink inn] but after keeping it a few years, he, in 1651, sold out to Smith his trading house, his two big guns, &c.

[3 Mass. Hist. Coll. vols i. and ii.

The Smiths afterwards made additional purchases of the Indians. * * * * *

Smith's was the first purchase, but there was not much done towards the settlement of the country, by the whites, until the Petaquamscutt purchase some time after.—Callender.   [Extracted from Potter's Hist. Narragansett.

No. II.—[p. 37.]

[From the New York Gazette, January, 1770.]

To the Printer.   Sir,—In the New York Gazette, under the Philadelphia head, I find the following article, dated the 8th instant.   Last Friday morning died, in an
advanced age, Mrs. Sarah Goddard, late of Providence, in
Rhode-Island; and yesterday her remains were interred
in Christ Church burying ground, in this city, attended
by a number of respectable inhabitants.   She was the
widow of Dr. Giles Goddard, formerly of New-London,
in Connecticut.

This is so very short and simple an account of the decease of a very amiable lady, who was really an ornament
and honor to her sex, that in justice to her character, I
think myself obliged, though no relation to the family,
nor very intimately acquainted, to mention the following
particulars which have come to my knowledge.

Her ancestors were among the first settlers of the colony of Rhode-Island, persons in affluent circumstances,
and of the most respectable characters.   Her father, Mr.
Lodowick Updike, was remarkable for his hospitality, and
his house was a noted asylum for the distressed.   She
was, together with her brother, [Daniel Updike, Esq.,
late Attorney General of that colony,] educated in her
father's house, by the best tutors that could be procured.
She discovered an extraordinary genius and taste for, and
made a most surprising progress in, most kinds of useful
and polite learning, not only in the accomplishments to
which a female is usually confined, but in languages, and
several branches of the mathematics.   Her acquaintance

and connections were among the most respectable people of Rhode-Island, Connecticut and Boston. In the last of these places she resided some time of her youth. Afterwards, in New London, she lived many years with her husband, Dr. G. Goddard, who about thirteen years ago left her a widow, with two children, not grown up, a son and a daughter. After this, she continued in New London for seven or eight years, which she spent in a constant practice of all the social duties, and a series of virtuous efforts, manifesting true wisdom and fortitude.

Having taken a liking to the printing business, through her means, her son was instructed in it, and settled in a printing house, in the town of Providence, to which place she soon after removed, and became a partner with him in the business, which was carried on several years to general acceptance, the last two years under their more immediate joint management and direction ; the credit of the paper was greatly promoted by her virtue, ingenuity and abilities.

Her son having an opportunity of engaging in a much more extensive business in Philadelphia, where advantageous offers were made him, removed there ; and about two years after, she was induced by maternal affection to quit her settlement and acquaintance in Providence, where she was greatly respected, and live with her son in Philadelphia, to which place she removed about fourteen months ago.

Her uncommon attainments in literature, were the least valuable parts of her character. Her conduct through all the changing, trying scenes of life, was not only unblam-

22*

able, but exemplary ;—a sincere piety and unaffected humility, an easy, agreeable cheerfulness and affability, an entertaining, sensible and edifying conversation, and a prudent attention to all the duties of domestic life, endeared her to all of her acquaintances, especially in the relations of wife, parent, friend and neighbor. The death of such a person is a public loss ; an irreparable one to her children.

No. III.—[p. 39.]
Trial of the Pirates.

"Two Pirate sloops, the Ranger and the Fortnne, which had committed various piracies on the high seas, being in company on the 8th of May, 1723, captured the ship Amsterdam Merchant, John Welland, Master, the day after which capture, they plundered and sunk the ship, and on the 6th day of June, in Latitude 39, they took a Virginia sloop, rifled her and let her go, who the next day fell in with his Majesties ship the Grey Hound, Captain Solgard, of 20 guns, to whom they related the circumstances of their late capture and release. Captain Solgard immediately pursued, and on the 10th came up with the Pirate sloops, about 14 leagues south of the east end of Long Island—who mistaking him for a merchant ship, immediately gave chase and soon commenced firing on the Grey Hound, under a black flag, but then hauled down the black flag and hoisted the red flag. The Grey Hound succeeded in capturing one of the sloops after having seven men wounded, but the other Pirate escaped. The Grey Hound came with the prize into the harbor of Newport, and the Pirates, 36 in number were committed for trial ; 26 were

Gravelly Point, opposite the town, on the 19th of July, 1723. After execution, their bodies were carried to Goat or Fort Island, and buried on the shore, between high and low water mark.

As this was perhaps the most extensive execution of Pirates that ever took place at one time in the colonies, and as it may be curious to know the manner and form of the proceedings on this trial, as the same was published at the time, it is added in the appendix."

[Bull's Memoirs.

TRIALS

OF THIRTY-SIX PERSONS FOR PIRACY, &c.

Twenty-eight of them upon full evidence were found guilty, and the rest acquitted.

At a Court of Admiralty, for trial of Pirates, held at Newport, within his Majesty's Colony of Rhode Island and Providence Plantations in America, on the 10th, 11th, and 12th days of July, Anno Domini, 1723, pursuant to his Majesty's Commission, founded on an act of Parliament, made on the 11th and 12th years of King William the Third, entitled *An act for the more effectual suppression of Piracy*, and made perpetual by an act of the Sixth of King George.

Boston: Printed and sold by Samuel Kneeland, in Queen street, below the Prison, 1723.

———

At a Court of Admiralty, for the trial of Pirates, held at the Town House in Newport, in the Colony of Rhode Island and Providence Plantations, the 10th of July, in ninth year of his Majesties reign A. D., 1723.

PRESENT.

The Honorable WILLIAM DUMMER, Esquire, Lieutenant Governor and Commander-in-Chief of the Province of the Massachusetts Bay, President of the Court.

The Honoroble SAMUEL CRANSTON, Esquire, Governor of the Colony of Rhode Island, &c

NATHANIEL PAINE,
ADDISON DAVENPORT,   } Esquires of the Council of
THOMAS FITCH,   Massachusetts Bay,
SPENCER PHIPPS,

THOMAS LECHMORE, Esq., Surveyor General of North America.

NATHANIEL KAY, Esq., Collector of the Colony of Rhode Island, Commissioner appointed by his Majesties Commission, for the trial of the Pirates.

First Proclamation was made, commanding silence upon pain of imprisonment, whilst the Parliament and his Majesties Commission for the trial of Pirates were reading.

Then the said Court were publickly and solemnly opened

act, after which his Honor administered the same oath to

The Court appointed Richard Ward, sole Notary Public

said Court.

And Jahleel Brenton, Jun., Esq., Provost Marshal of said Court.

Then a warrant issued out to the Provost Marshal, to bring the prisoners into Court, to-morrow morning, at eight of the clock.

Then the crier made Proclamation for all persons that could give evidence for the King against the prisoners to be tried, to come into Court, and they should be heard.

Then the court adjourned till to-morrow morning, eight of the clock in the forenoon, July 11th day, 1723.

The Court met according to adjournment, and was opened by three Proclamations.

PRESENT.

The Hon. William Dummer, Esq., &c., President.

The Hon. Samuel Cranston, Esq., &c.

Nathaniel Paine,
Addison Davenport,   Esquires of the Council of
Thomas Fitch,   Massachusetts Bay.
Spencer Phipps,

John Menzies, Esq., Judge of the Vice Admirality &c.

Thomas Lechmore, Esq., Surveyor General.

Nathaniel Kay, Esq., Collector of Rhode Island.

John Menzies, Esq., being appointed Commissioner, had the oath administered to him by the President.

Then Charles Harris, Thomas Powell, John Wilson, Thomas Linnicar, Daniel Hyde, Stephen Mundon, Abraham Lacy, Edward Lawson, John Tomkins, Henry Burns, Francis Laughton, John Fitzgerald, William Studfield, Owen Rice, William Read, Thomas Hugget, Peter Cues, Thomas Jones, William Jones, Edward Eaton, John Brown, Joseph Sound, John Brown, James Sprinkly, Charles Church, John Waters, Thomas Mumford, Indian, and John Kencate, Doctor, were brought to the bar, and arraigned upon the articles exhibited against them (and others,) for piracy, robbery, and felony.

The Register read the articles in these words following:

At a Court of Admiralty for trial of Pirates, held at Newport in the Colony of Rhode Island, &c. the 10th day of July, A. D. 1723.

Articles of Piracy, Robbery and Felony, exhibited then and there against Charles Harris, Thomas Powell, John

Wilson, Thomas Linnicar, William Blades, Daniel Hyde, Stephen Mundon, Abraham Lacy, Edward Lawson, John Tompkins, Henry Barnes, Francis Laughton, John Fitzgerald, William Studfield, Owen Rice, William Read, Thomas Hugget, Peter Cues, Thomas Jones, William Jones, Edward Eaton, Joseph Swetser, John Brown, Joseph Sound, Charles Church, John Waters, Thomas Mumford, Indian, and John Kencate, Doctor.

You stand here accused of Felony, Piracy, and Robbery. First, for that you, the said Charles Harris, with the other Prisoners, (and divers others,) about the eighth day of May last, in the latitude 22 D. North, off cape Antonio, by force and arms upon the High Sea, (within the jurisdiction of the Admirality of Great Britain,) piratically and feloniously did surprise, seize, and take ship Amsterdam Merchant, whereof John Welland was then commander or master, of the burthen of one hundred tons, belonging to his Majesty's good subjects.

And out of her, then and there, within the jurisdiction aforesaid, feloniously and piratically, did take and carry away three barrels of beef of the value of seven pounds, some quantities of gold and silver, of the value of one hundred and fifty pounds, one negro man, slave, named Dick, of the value of fifty pounds. And also, then and there, did piratically and feloniously sink the said ship, of the value of one thousand pounds, and cut off the said Welland's right ear.

Secondly, That you the said Charles Harris, Thomas Powell, John Wilson, Thomas Linnicar, William Blades, Daniel Hyde, Stephen Mundon, Abraham Lacy, Edward Lawson, John Tompkins, Henry Barnes, Francis Laughton, John Fitzgerald, William Studfield, Owen Rice, William Read, Thomas Hugget, Peter Cues, Thomas Jones, William Jones, Edward Eaton, Joseph Swetser, John Brown, James Sprinkly, John Brown, Joseph Sound, Charles Church, John Waters, Thomas Mumford, Indian, and John Kencate, (with divers others,) on or about the tenth day of June last, fourteen leagues to the southward of the east end of Long Island, by force and arms upon the High Sea, within the jurisdiction of the Admiralty aforesaid, in a hostile manner, did feloniously and piratically attack his Majesty's ship the Grey Hound, Captain Peter Solgard, commander, and wounded seven of his men.

All which aforesaid piracies, robberies and felonies, were by you, and each of you, done and committed in manner as aforesaid, contrary to the statutes and laws in that case made and provided.

John Valentine, Advocate General for the King.

To which articles the said Charles Harris, with the other prisoners before mentioned, brought to the bar, severally pleaded not guilty.

And Charles Harris, Thomas Linnicar, Daniel Hyde, Stephen Mundon, Abraham Lacy, Edward Lawson, John Tompkins, Francis Lawson, John Fitzgerald, William Studfield, Owen Rice, William Read, John Wilson, and Henry Barnes, were ordered to be tried this forenoon. And Thomas Powell, Thomas Hugget, Peter Cues, Thomas Jones, William Jones, Edward Eaton, John Brown, James Sprinkly, John Brown, Joseph Sound, Charles Church, John Waters, Thomas Mumford, Indian, and John Kencate, Doctor, were remanded (by the court,) to prison, to be brought on to trial, as they should order.

Then the Advocate General proceeded. May it please your honor, and the rest of the honorable Judges of this Court—

them committed upon the High Sea, to which they have severally pleaded not guilty.

ery,) committed within the jurisdiction of the

And a pirate is described to be, one who to enrich himself either by surprise or open force, sets upon merchants, and others trading by sea, to spoil them of their goods and treasure, often times by sinking their vessels as the case will come out before you.

This sort of criminals are engaged in a perpetual war with every individual, with every state, christian or infidel; they have no country, but by the nature of their guilt, separate themselves, renouncing the benefit of all lawful society, to commit these heinous offences : the Romans therefore justly styled them *Hostes humani Generis*, enemies of all mankind; and indeed they are enemies, and armed against themselves, a kind of *felons de se*, importing something more than a natural death.

These unhappy men, satiated with the number and notoriety of their crimes, had filled up the measure of their guilt, when by the Providence of Almighty God, and through the valor and conduct of Captain Solgard, they are delivered up to the sword of justice.

23

The Roman emperors in their edict, made this piece of service, so eminent for the public good, as meritorious as any act of piety, or religious worship whatsoever.

And 'twill doubtless be said, for the honor of this colony, (though of late scandalously reproached to have combined with pirates!) and be evinced by the process and event of this affair, that such flagitious persons, find as little countenance and shelter, and as much justice at Rhode Island, as in any other part of his Majesty's dominions.

But your time is more precious than my words; I will not mispend it, in attempting to set forth the aggravations of this complex crime, big with enormity, nor in declaring the mischiefs, and evil tendencies of it; for you better know these things before I mention them, and I consider to whom I speak and that the judgement is your honors. I shall therefore call the king's evidences to prove the several facts, as so many distinct acts of piracy, charged on the prisoners; not by light circumstances and presentations, not by strained and unfounded conjectures, but by clear and positive evidence, and then I doubt not, since for 'tis the interest of mankind, that these crimes should be punished; your honors will do justice to the prisoners, this Colony, and the rest of the world, in pronouncing them guilty, and in passing sentence upon them according to law.

The king's evidences being sworn and examined, deposed as follows :—

John Welland of Boston, mariner, to the first article, charged, that upon the eighth day of May, 1723, being in the aforesaid ship, the Amsterdam Merchant, and master of her, off Cape Antonio, he was chased by two sloops, whereof one of them came up with him, and hoisted a blue flag, and took him. She was called the Ranger, a pirate under the command of Edward Low, who was in the other sloop that chased him, and that the deponent was ordered on board the Ranger, where he went aboard with four of his men, and the quarter-master examined him, how much money he had aboard, and he told him about £150, in gold and silver, which they took out of the vessel; and after he had been aboard the Ranger sloop, three hours, he was carried on board the sloop Fortune, where Low was, where he was very much abused, having several wounds with a cutlass, and at last they cut off his right ear; and the next day following, after they had taken out of his ship, one negro, some beef, and other things, they sunk the ship, and the day after he was taken, the said pirate took one Captain Eastwick, of Piscataqua, on board of whom they afterwards put this deponent and dismissed him; the pirates were all harnessed with weapons, except Thomas Jones.

And also further deposed, that Henry Barnes, now one of the prisoners at the bar, was forced out of his ship at the said time and was very low and weak, and that the said Barnes being ordered by the pirates to go from vessel to vessel with them, (that is their prizes,) when he got on board of Captain Eastwick, he endeavored to get away, and hid himself; and the pirates threatened to burn the ship, unless they discovered the said Barnes, whereupon the said Barnes was compelled to go on board the pirate ship.

John Ackin, mariner, and late mate of the ship Amsterdam Merchant, deposed that he was mate of the above said ship, taken as aforesaid, by Low, the pirate, and his crew in the two sloops, Fortune and the Ranger, and that the said pirate forced from out the said ship Amsterdam Merchant, one Henry Barnes, now a prisoner at the bar, who cried and took on very much, and desired this deponent to acquaint his three sisters, living in Barbadoes, that he was a forced man, and also very sick and weak at the said time.

John Mudd, ship carpenter, and late carpenter on board the aforesaid ship Amsterdam Merchant, being sworn and examined, deposeth, that he was a carpenter on board the said ship, when she was taken by Low's company, in the sloops Fortune and Ranger, off Cape Antonio, and that he was carried on board sloop Ranger; and most of the pirates were harnessed, that is armed with guns, &c.

Captain Peter Solgard, commander of his Majesty's ship the Grey Hound, deposed, that being cruising in the said ship, the Grey Hound, in or near the latitude 39, d. m., on the 7th day of June last, he spoke with the master of a Virginian ship, who informed him, that the day before he had been taken by two pirate sloops, that rifled his ship; in the evening they left him, and steered to the northward, as he believed, for Block Island; whereupon Captain Solgard immediately pursued them, and on the tenth, being about fourteen leagues to the southard of the east end of Long Island, saw two sloops, which he concluded to be the pirates, and seemed some time to stand from them to encourage them to give him chase, which they did with sails and oars; when they came near they hoisted black flags, and fired each a shot, and soon afterwards they hauled down their black flags and hoisted red flags; then he hoisted his Majesties colors, and they began the engagement; the fire continued on both sides, near an

hour, when they perceiving themselves overpowered, put
away before the wind, and endeavored by rowing to make
their escape, and there being but little wind, he got out
his oars and pursued them; about three o'clock in the
afternoon he came near them again, when they renewed
the engagement, about four, he got between them, and
shot down their main sails, which obliged them soon after
to call for quarters; he then immediately sent on board the
Lieutenant, and took out the prisoners now at the bar,

action they seemed to use their utmost endeavors to annoy
his Majesty's ship, and wounded seven of his men, and
did much damage to her rigging and sails.

Edward Smith, Lieutenant, of his Majesty's ship Grey
Hound, deposed the same that Captain Solgard did.

Archibald Fisher, Surgeon, of the Grey Hound man-of-
war, deposed, that there were seven of the Grey Hound's
men wounded in the fight, by the two pirate sloop companies, in the engagement between the Grey Hound
man-of-war and them, but none mortal.

William Marsh, mariner, being duly sworn, deposed
and said, that sometime last January, he was taken in the
West Indies, by Low's company, in a schooner and sloop,
near Boniase, and that he saw on board of the schooner,
Francis Laughton and William Read, and on board of the
sloop, he saw Charles Harris, Edward Lawson, Daniel
Hyde, and John Fitzgerald, all prisoners at the bar, and
that Gerald asked him if he would seek his fortune with
him.

23*

After the witnesses had been severally examined, the prisoners at the bar were asked whether they had any thing to say in their own defence, whereto they answered and said, they were forced men on board of Low, and did nothing voluntarily, but as they were compelled.

ADVOCATE GENERAL.

Your Honors, I doubt not have observed the weakness and vanity of the defence which has been made by the prisoners at the bar, and that the articles (containing indisputable flagrant acts of piracy) are supported against each of them. Their impudence and unfortunate mistake in attacking his Majesty's ship, tho' to us fortunate, and of great service to the neighboring governments; their malicious and cruel assault upon Capt. Welland, not only in the spoiling of his goods, but what is much more, the cutting of his right ear, a crime of that nature and barbarity which can never be repaired.

Their plea of constraint, or force (in the mouth of every pirate) can be of no avail to them, for if that would jusify or excuse, no pirate, would ever be convicted nor even any profligate person of his own account offend against the moral law; if it were asked, would it be hard to answer who offered the violence? It's apparent they forced, or pursuaded one another, or rather the compulsion proceeded of their own corrupt and avaricous inclinations; but if there was the least semblance of truth in the plea; it might come out in proof that the prisoners or some of them did manifest their uneasiness and sorrow, to some of the persons whom they have surprised and robbed; but the contrary of that is plain from Mr. Marsh's evidence, that the prisoners were so far from a dislike, or regretting their wicked course of life, that they were for increasing their number, by inviting him to join them, and so seemed resolved to live and die by their calling, or for it, as their fate is like to be. And now seeing that the facts are as evident as proof by testimony can make them, I doubt not your honors will declare the prisoners to be guilty.

Then the prisoners were taken away from the bar, and the court was cleared and in private.

Then the court having duly and maturely weighed and considered the evidences against the prisoners, unanimously agreed and voted that Charles Harris, Thomas Linnicar, Daniel Hyde, Stephen Mundon, Abraham Lacy, Edward Lawson, John Tomkins, Francis Laughton, John Fitzgerald, William Studfield, Owen Rice, and William Read, were guilty of the piracies, robberies and felouies exhibited against them at this court; and that John Wilson, and Henry Barns were not guilty.

And then the court adjourned to two of the clock in the afternoon of said day.

The court met and opened by proclamation, according to adjournment, and the aforesaid prisoners that were tried in the forenoon, were brought to the bar again.

And the President acquainted them, that the court by a unanimous voice, had found the aforesaid Charles Harris, Thomas Linnican, Daniel Hyde, Stephen Mundon, Abraham Lacy, Edward Lawson, John Tomkins, Francis Laughton, John Fitzgerald, William Studfield, Owen Rice, and William Read, guilty of piracies, robberies and felonies according to the articles exhibited against them, and asked them whether any of them had any thing to say, why sentence of death should not be passed upon them for their said offences.

And the prisoners offering nothing material, the President pronounced sentence against them in the following words:—

You Charles Harris, Thomas Linnican, Daniel Hyde, Stephen Mundon, Abraham Lacy, Edward Lawson, John Tomkins, Francis Laughton, John Fitzgerald, William Studfield, Owen Rice, and William Read, are to go from hence to the place from which they came, and from thence to the place of execution, and there you and each of you, are to be hanged by the neck until you are dead, and the Lord have mercy upon your souls.

And the President then pronounced the said John Wilson and Henry Barns not guilty.

Then the court ordered Thomas Hugget, Peter Cues, Thomas Jones, William Jones, Edward Eaton, John Brown, James Sprinkly, John Brown, Joseph Sound, Charles Church John Waters, and Thomas Mumford, Indian, who were arraigned in the morning, and had severally pleaded not guilty, to be brought accordingly to the bar, and they were brought, and William Blades was also brought, and articles of piracies, robberies and felonies exhibited against him, read to him in the same words as before mentioned, whereunto he pleaded not guilty.

ADVOCATE GENERAL.

May it please your Honors,—The prisoners before the court are a part of that miserable crew of men already under sentence of death

The articles, the crimes, and evidences being the same

with those of their brethren, and their guilt equal, I doubt not they will meet with the like condemnation.

The king's evidences being called and sworn, depose as followeth.

John Welland deposeth, that he was master of the ship Amsterdam, merchant, in the month of May last past, and that on the eighth of May, he was taken by Low and Company, pirates, in two sloops, off Cape Antonio, who used him as afore sworn, and that he saw Charles Church, John Waters, Edward Eaton, William Blades, Thomas Mumford, Indian, and Thomas Jones, a lad, on board the Ranger; that the day after he was taken, the said pirate took one Captain Eastwick, of Piscataqua; the pirates were all harnessed, (as they called it, viz. armed,) except Thomas Jones, who was a lad on board.

John Ackin, late mate of the ship Amsterdam Merchant, deposed, that he was taken in the ship Amsterdam Merchant, by Low and crew, as aforesaid, and that John Waters and Thomas Jones, a lad, prisoners at the bar, were then on board one of the pirate sloops called the Ranger, that Waters demanded what sum they had, and that Thomas Jones was not armed as he knows of.

John Mudd, late carpenter of the ship Amsterdam Merchant, deposed, that the ship aforesaid, was taken in manner as aforesaid, by the aforesaid Low, and crew of pirates, and that he well remembers Joseph Sound, Thomas Jones and Thomas Mumford, Indian, on board the Ranger, when the said Joseph Sound, and most of the company were harnessed, viz: armed; and said Sound took his buttons out of his sleeves, but that Thomas Jones was not in arms as he knew of.

Benjamin Wickham, of Newport, mariner, deposed, that on the tenth of March, last, he was in the bay of Hondoras, on board of a sloop, Jeremiah Clark, master, Low and Lowder's companies, being pirates, took the aforesaid sloop, and that this deponent, then having the small pox, was by John Waters, one of the prisoners at the bar, carried on board another vessel; and that he begged of some of the company, two shirts to shirt himself, the said Waters said *damn* him, he would beg the vessel too, but at other times he was very civil; and the deponent further saith, he saw William Blades now prisoner at the bar, among them.

William Marsh, deposed, that he was taken in manner as aforesaid, and that John Brown, the tallest man, was on board the schooner, and the said Brown, told him, he had rather be in a tight vessel than a leaky one, and that he was not forced.

Captain Solgard and Lieutenant Smith, deposed, that they took the sloop Ranger, at time, place, and manner as aforesaid; and that the prisoners at the bar, were taken from on board her.

Henry Barnes, mariner, being duly sworn, deposed, that he being on board sloop Ranger, during her engagement with the Grey Hound, man-of-war, saw all the prisoners at the bar, on board the said sloop Ranger, and that he saw John Brown the shortest, in arms, that Thomas Mumford, Indian, was only as a servant on board.

John Wilson, being duly sworn and interrogated, deposed, that the major part of the prisoners, now at the bar, were active on board the sloop Ranger, in attacking and engaging the Grey Hound, man-of-war, and that Edward Eaton, was hart in the knee, by by a great gun; saw all the prisoners at the bar, on board the said sloop Ranger, in attacking and engaging the Grey Hound, and that I saw John Brown, the shortest, in arms, that Thomas Mumford, Indian, was only as servant on board.

After the witnesses had been severally examined, the prisoners at the bar, were asked whether they had any thing to say in their own defence.

William Blades, he was forced on board of Low, about eleven months ago, and never signed their articles, and that he had, when taken, about ten or twelve pounds, and only took what they gave him, never shared with them.

Thomas Hugget, said he was one of Captain Mercy's men, on board the Giuiza and in the West Indies, was put on board of Low, but never shared with them, and they gave him about twenty-one pounds.

Peter Cues, says, that on the twenty-third or twenty-fourth of January last, he belonged to one Layal, in a sloop of Antigua, and was then taken by Low, and detained ever since, but never shared with them, and had about ten or twelve pounds when taken, which they gave him.

Thomas Jones, says, he is a lad of about seventeen years of age, and was by Low and company, taken out of Captain Edwards, at Newfoundland, and kept by Low ever since.

William Jones, says, he was taken out of Captain Ester, at the Bay of Honduras, the beginning of April last, by Low and Lowder's, and that he never shared with them, nor signed the articles till compelled, three weeks after he was taken; and the said Jones owned he had eleven pounds of the quarter-master at one time, and eight pounds at another.

Edward Eaton, says, that he was taken by Low in the Bay of Hondoras, about the beginning of March, and kept with him by force ever since.

John Brown, the tallest, says, that on the ninth of October last, he was taken out of the Liverpool Merchant, at the Cape De Verde, by Captain Low, who beat him black and blue to make him sign the articles; and from the Cape De Verde, they cruised upon the coast of Brazil about eleven weeks, and from thence to the West Indies, and he was on board of the Ranger at the taking of Welland.

James Sprinkly, says, he was forced out of a ship, at the Cape De Verdes, by Low, in October last, and by him compelled to sign the articles, but never shared with them.

John Brown, the shortest, says, he is about seventeen years old, and was in October last, at the Cape De Verdes, taken out of a ship by Low, and kept there ever since, and that the quarter-master gave him about forty shillings, and the people aboard three pounds.

Joseph Sound, says, he was taken from Providence, three months ago, by Low and company, and detained by force ever since.

Charles Church, says, he was taken out of the Sycamore Gally, at the Cape De Verdes, Captain Scott, commander, about seven or eight months ago, by Captain Low, never shared, but the quarter-master gave him about fourteen pounds.

John Waters, says, he was taken by Low, on the twenty-ninth of June last, out of —————, and they compelled him to take charge of a watch, and that he had thirteen pistoles when taken, which was given him, and that he said in the time of the engagement with his Majesty's ship, they had better strike, for they would have better quarters.

Thomas Mumford, Indian, says he was a servant, a fishing the last year, and was taken out of a fishing sloop with five other Indians, off Nantucket, by Low and Company, and that they hanged two of the Indians at Cape Sables, and that he was kept by Low ever since, and had about six bits when taken.

And then the prisoners were taken from the bar, and secured, and the court in private.

Then the court maturely weighed and considered the evidences and the prisoners case, and unanimously found William Blades, Thomas Hugget, Peter Cues, William Jones, Edward Eaton, John Brown, James Sprinkly, John Brown, Joseph Sound, Charles Church, and John Waters, all guilty of piracy, robbery, and felony, according to the articles exhibited against them.

And by a unanimous voice found Thomes Jones, and Thomas Mumford, Indian, not guilty.

The aforesaid prisoners were brought to the bar, and the President acquainted them, that the court by a unanimous voice, had found the aforesaid, William Blades, Thomas Hugget, Peter Cues, William Jones, Edward Eaton, John Brown, James Sprinkly, John Brown, Joseph Sound, Charles Church, and John Waters, all guilty of

24

the piracies, robberies and felonies, according to the articles exhibited against them; and asked them whether any of them had any thing to say why the sentence of death should not pass upon them for their offences.

And the prisoners offering nothing material, the President pronounced sentence of death against them in the following words:—

You, William Blades, Thomas Hugget, Peter Cues, William Jones, Edward Eaton, John Brown, Joseph Sound, Charles Church, John Brown, James Sprinkley, and John Waters, are to go from hence to the place from whence you came, and from thence to the place of execution, and there you and each of you shall be hanged by the neck, until you are dead, and the Lord have mercy on your souls.

And the President pronounced the said Thomas Jones, and Thomas Mumford, Indian, not guilty.

Then the court adjourned until to-morrow morning, at eight of the clock in the forenoon.

JULY, the twelth day, 1723.

The court met according to adjournment, and was opened by proclamation.

Present, the HON. WILLIAM, DUMMER, Esq. Lieutenant Governor and Commander-in-chief, of the Massachusetts Bay.

The HON. SAMUEL CRANSTON, Esq., Governor of Rhode Island.

NATHANIEL PAINE,
ADDINGTON DAVENPORT,   Esquires, of the Council
THOMAS FITCH,   of the Massachusetts Bay
SPENCER PHIPP,

JOHN MENZIES, Esq., Judge of the Vice Admiralty.

NATHANIEL KAY, Esq., Collector of Rhode Island.

Ordered that John Kencate, Doctor, who was arraigned yesterday be brought to the bar, accordingly he was brought to the bar.

ADVOCATE GENERAL.

May it please your Honors,—The next person brought in judgment before this Honorable Court, is the Doctor of the piratical crew; and although it may be said, he said, he used no arms, was not harnessed (as they term it,) but was a forced man; yet if he received part of their plunder, was not under constant durance, did at any time approve, or join in their villanies, his guilt is at least equal to the rest; the Doctor being adored among them, as the pirates God, for in him they chiefly confided for their cure and life, and in this trust and dependence, it is, that they enterprize those horrid depredations, not to be heightened by aggravation, or lessened by excuse.

The Kings evidences being called, sworn and interogated, deposed as follows:

John Welland, deposeth, he was taken as aforesaid, and that he saw the Doctor, aboard the Ranger; he seemed not to rejoice when he was taken, but solitary; and he was informed on board, he was a forced man, and that he never signed the articles as he heard of; and was not on board the deponents ship.

John Ackin, mate, and John Mudd, Carpenter, swore that they saw the prisoner at the bar, walking forwards and backwards, disconsolately, on board the Ranger.

Benjamin Wickham, deposed, that he doth not know the prisoner at the bar, by sight, but that while he was at the bay, under confinement, with said crew of pirates, there came a man on board the vessel, whom they called the Doctor, who drank, and was merry with some of the pirates then there, and told him, the deponent, he would send him something to take, but sent it not.

Captain Peter Solgard, commander of his Majesty's ship Grey Hound, and Edward Smith, Lieutenant, on board ship, deposed, that the prisoner at the bar was on board the sloop Ranger, when taken, in manner and time as aforesaid.

Archibald Fisher, physician and surgeon, on board the said Grey Hound, man-of-war, deposed, that when the prisoner at the bar was taken and brought aboard the King's ship, he searched his medicaments, and the instruments, and found but very few medicants, and the instruments very mean and bad.

John Wilson, Henry Barns, and Thomas Jones, severally deposed, that the prisoner at the bar was forced on board by Low, and that he never signed articles as they knew or heard, but used to spend great part of his time in reading, and was very courtous to the prisoners taken by Low and company, and that he never shared with them as they knew or heard of.

After the witnesses were duly interrogated, the court asked the prisoner whether he had any thing to say in his defence, and if he had he might speak.

John Kencate, Dr., saith, he was surgeon of the Syca-more-Galley, Andrew Scott, master, and was taken out of the said ship in September last, at Bonavista, one of the Cape De Verde Islands, by Low and company, who detained him ever since, and that he never shared with them, or signed articles.

The prisoner was taken from the bar, and the court cleared.

Then the court examined and considered the evidences, and pleas for the king, and the prisoners case, with great care, and by a unanimous voice, found the said John Kencate, Doctor, not guilty.

Then the court was again opened, and the said prisoner, John Kencate, was brought to the bar, and the president pronounced him not guilty.

Ordered, that Thomas Powell, who was arraigned, and pleaded not guilty, yesterday, and Joseph Swetser, who was articled against, yesterday, in the aforesaid articles, but not arraigned, and Joseph Libbey, articled against since, with others, for piracies, robberies, and felonies, be brought to the bar, and they were brought to the bar accordingly.

When the Register read the aforesaid articles exhibited against Joseph Swetser, in the words aforesaid, to which he pleaded not guilty.

Then the Register read the articles exhibited against

Then the Register asked the said Joseph Libbey, whether he was guilty of the articles exhibited against him, or not guilty, and the prisoner, Joseph Libbey, pleaded not guilty.

Whereupon the Register bid the said Thomas Powell, Joseph Swetser, and Joseph Libbey attend to their trial.

ADVOCATE GENERAL.

May it please your Honors,—The three prisoners at the bar, charged for the same crime, and tried together

24*

at their desire in hope to distinguish themselves by their innocency, from the rest under condemnation, will I doubt not find their mistake, in their conviction, and in the sentence they may justly expect to hear from this honorable court.

Then the king's evidences being called, sworn and interrogated, deposed as follows:

John Welland, late master of the ship Amsterdam Merchant, deposed, that when he was taken as aforesaid, by Low and company, he saw Joseph Swetser, and Thomas Powell, aboard sloop Ranger, and that they were harnessed on board the sloop.

John Ackin, late mate of the said ship, deposed, that he saw Joseph Swetser, harnessed on board the sloop Ranger, at the taking of Captain Welland, by Low, and he saw Thomas Powell on board, but not harnessed.

John Mudd, late carpenter of the ship Amsterdam Merchant, deposed the same as Ackin.

William Marsh, deposed, that Thomas Powell, a prisoner at the bar, was on board of Low, the pirate, some time in January last, when this deponent was taken by Low, and that Powell seemed to be a brisk, stirring, active man amongst them, and told the deponent they always kept a barrel of powder ready, to blow up the sloop rather than be taken, and that the said Powell searched the deponents pockets for gold and silver, in the great cabin, on board of Low.

John Kencate, deposed, that during his being on board of Low, the pirate, he well knew Thomas Powell, Joseph Swetser, and Joseph Libbey, now prisoners at the bar, and that Thomas Powell, acted as gunner on board the

Ranger, and that he went on board several vessels, taken by Low and company, and that Joseph Libbey was an active man aboard the Ranger, and used to go on board vessels they took and plundered, and that he saw him fire several times, and the deponent further deposed, that Joseph Swetser, now prisoner at the bar, was on board the pirate Low, and that he has seen him armed, saw him use them, and that the said Swetser used often to get alone by himself, from amongst the rest of the crew, he was melancholy, and refused to go on board any vessels by them taken, and got out of their way. And the deponent further saith, that on that day, as they engaged the man-of-war, Low proposed to attack the man-of-war, first by firing his great guns, then a volley of small arms, heave in their powder flasks, and board her in his sloop, and the Ranger to board over the Fortune, and that no one on board the Ranger disagreed to it as he knows of, for most approved it by their words, and the others were silent.

Thomas Jones, deposed, that he well knew the prisoners at the bar, and that Thomas Powell acted as gunner, on board the Ranger; and Joseph Libbey was a stirring, active man among them, and used to go aboard vessels to plunder, and that Joseph Swetser was very dull aboard, and at Cape Antonio, he cried to Dunnell, to let him go ashore, who refused, and asked him to drink a dram, but Swetser went down into the hold and cried a good part of day, and that Low refused to let him go, but brought him and tied him to the mast, and threatened to whip him; and he saw him armed, but never use his arms as he knows of; and that Swetser was sick when they engaged the man-of-war, though he assisted in rowing the vessel.

John Wilson, deposed, he knows the prisoners at the bar, to be all on board the Ranger, and Thomas Powell, was gunner of her; and the sabbath-day before taken, the said Powell told the deponent, he wished he was ashore at Long Island, and they two went to the head of the mast, and Powell said to him, I wish you and I were both ashore here stark naked; and he deposed that he never saw Joseph Swetser in arms, while on board; but he and Powell received about twenty-five pounds from the quarter-master. That the next day after the deponent was taken by Low, Joseph Swetser told him that he was a forced man, and wished he had his liberty, as he had about fourteen months ago, and he was resolved to run away the first opportunity he had.

Henry Barns, deposed, that Joseph Swetser was very civil on board the sloop Ranger, to such prisoners as was taken, and that they had no engagement after the deponent was on board, and that Joseph Libbey, was armed, and went on board several vessels taken by them and plundered.

Thomas Mumford, Indian, (not speaking good English, Abishai Folger, was sworn interpeter,) deposed, that Thomas Powell, Joseph Libbey, and Joseph Swetser, were all on board of Low, the pirate, that he saw Powell have a gun when they took vessels, but never saw him fire, he saw him go on board of a vessel once, but brought nothing from her as he saw, he see him once strike a negro, but never a white man. And he saw Joseph Libbey, once go on board a vessel by them taken, and brought away from her one pair of Stockings; and that Joseph Swetser cooked on board with him sometimes, and sometimes they made him hand the sails; once he saw the said Swetser clean a gun, but not fire it, and Swetser once told him that he wanted to get ashore from among them, and said, if the man-of-war should take them they would hang him; and in the engagement of the man-of-war, Swetser sat unarmed in the range of the sloop's mast, and some little time before the said engagement, he asked Low to let him have his liberty, and go ashore, but was refused.

Captain Peter Solgard, commander of the Grey Hound, man-of-war, deposed, that all the prisoners now at the bar, were by him taken on board the Ranger on the tenth of June last, in manner as aforesaid, and that he had seven men wounded in the engagement.

Edward Smith, Lieutenant of the said man-of-war, deposed the same.

After the witnesses were severally examined. as aforesaid, the court told the prisoners, if they had any thing to say in their defence they might speak.

Thomas Powell, said he was taken by Lowther in the Bay of Hondoras, in the winter 1721–2, and by him turned on board of Low, and detained by force ever since.

Joseph Libbey, said, he was a forced man, and was detained by Low, produced an advertisement of it.

Joseph Swetser says, he was taken by Lowther about a year ago, and forced on board by Low, and detained there against his will ever since; that he never shared with them, but had of the quarter-master about twelve pounds, and to prove his being forced, produced an advertisement.

Advocate General.

May it please your Honors,—The prisoners, notwithstanding their plea of not guilty, don't deny the facts, but insist upon their having done them, not of their own will and choice, but by constraint and necessity.

But it is evident that Powell and Libbey were first rate pirates, the former acting as gunner on board the sloop; and though Swetser has produced some witnesses as to the innocency of his conversation before he met with, and was forced by the pirates—he cannot be ignorant that he is not questioned for any of his good, but vile deeds. Probably, at the first, he might act with some reluctancy, till by the repetition of his crimes, he became hardened into vicious habits, (*nemo repente pessimus,*) and, it is in proof that he had a gun, received part of the spoil, and assisted in rowing when the sloop engaged the man of war, all, or any of which acts conducing to the main end, involves him in the same guilt. (*Facimus quos inguinat æquat.*) The attacking his Majesty's ship was a notorious piracy, though the pirates were overcome, and taken by the captain, who might have done justice upon them himself, by hanging them all up at the yardarm. The plea of necessity is dangerous in the latitude used by the prisoners; and may, after this rate, be extended to palliate the breach of the ten commandments.

Then the prisoners being taken away, and all withdrawn but the Register,

The court maturely weighed and considered the evidences, and the cases of the prisoners, and by a unanimous voice, found the said Thomas Powell and Joseph Libbey guilty of piracies, robberies and felonies, exhibited against them, and by a considerable plurality of voices found the said Joseph Swetser not guilty.

Then the prisoners were brought to the bar, and the President acquainted Thomas Powell and Joseph Libbey that they were, by a unanimous voice, found guilty of the piracies, robberies and felonies exhibited against them, and asked them if they had any thing to say why sentence of death should not pass upon them for their offences.

And the prisoners offering nothing material, the President pronounced sentence against them in the following words:

You Thomas Powell, and Joseph Libbey, are to go from hence to the place from whence you came, from thence to the place of execution, and there you, and each of you, are to be hanged up by the neck until you are dead, and the Lord have mercy on your souls.

Adjourned to two of the clock in the afternoon.

The court met according to adjournment, opened by proclamation, and ordered Thomas Hazel, John Bright, John Fletcher, Thomas Child and Patrick Cunningham to be brought to the bar, who were ordered to attend to the articles read against them, for piracies, robberies and felonies, which was read by the Register in the same words as to Joseph Libbey.

To which the said prisoners severally pleaded not guilty.

ADVOCATE GENERAL.

May it please your Honors,—The prisoners before you have been arraigned, have pleaded not guilty, and are the last of that miserable crew to be tried. If I make out their guilt, I shall not question your justice.

The king's evidences being called, sworn, and interrogated, deposed as follows:

John Welland, late master of the ship Amsterdam Merchant, deposed, that on the eighth day of May last, he was
taken off of Cape Antonio by Low and company, pirates,
in two sloops, the Fortune and Ranger, and after he had
been some time on board the Ranger he was sent on board
the Fortune, where Low was, where he had his right ear
cut off, and was wounded very much with a cutlass, and
turned down the hatches, where be lay bleeding for two
or three hours, with a sentinel over him; at last, he asked
Patrick Cunningham, (who he thought was the means of
saving his life,) a prisoner now at the bar, to get him a
dram, for he was almost spent, and Patrick Cunningham
got him some water; then he asked him for the doctor,
and Cunningham brought the doctor to him, and helped
the doctor to dress him, and said, they were so cruel they
could not subsist long; and said Welland also deposed,
that he saw John Bright and Thomas Hazel on board the
Ranger, and Thomas Hazel was harnessed with a gun.

John Ackin, late mate of the said ship Amsterdam Merchant, deposed, he saw Thomas Hazel, now a prisoner at
the bar, on board the Ranger at the time and place aforesaid.

John Midd, late carpenter of said ship, deposed, that
while he was prisoner on board the Ranger, he saw Thomas
Hazel, John Bright, and John Fletcher, and that Thomas
Hazel was harnessed.

William Marsh deposed, that when he was on board the
pirate, Low, by whom he was taken, as before deposed,
he saw Thomas Hazel on board the schooner, and John
Fletcher, now prisoner at the bar, a boy.

John Kcncate deposed, that Thomas Hazel, John Bright and Patrick Cunningham, prisoners at the bar, received shares on board the pirate sloop; and Hazel and Bright went on board several prizes and plundered. That Thomas Child was in arms with the rest in the engagement with the Greyhound man of war, and that John Fletcher was a boy on board, and no otherwise.

Henry Barnes deposed, that Thomas Hazel was harnessed in the engagement with the Greyhound man of war, and John Bright was the drummer, and beat upon his drum, on the round-house, in the engagement, and that Patrick Cunningham had a pistol in his hands at the same time.

John Wilson deposed, that John Bright was as brisk as any of them on board of the Ranger, and beat the drum on the round-house the day they engaged the man of war, and that John Fletcher was a boy on board of the sloop, and no otherwise.

John Swetser deposed, that John Bright was drummer, and beat upon the round-house in the engagement with the man of war; that Thomas Hazel had a pistol at the same time, and that Thomas Child came on board the Ranger, from the Fortune, but about three or four days before the said engagement, and rowed in the time of the said engagement.

Thomas Jones deposed, that on that day they engaged the Greyhound man of war, he saw Thomas Hazel bring his arms out of the gun-room, and saw and heard John Bright, the drummer, beat the drum upon the round-house, and Thomas Child employed at an oar rowing.

25

Captain Solgard, commander of his Majesty's ship Greyhound, deposed, that all the prisoners now at the bar were by him taken on board the sloop Ranger, on the tenth of June last, after some hours engagement, in manner aforesaid, and that he had several men wounded in the engagement.

Edward Smith, Lieutenant of the Greyhound man of war, deposed the same that Captain Solgard did.

After the witnesses were severally examined, as afore said, the court told the prisoners if they had any thing to say in their defence they might speak, and they should be heard.

Thomas Hazel said, he was taken from the Bay of Honduras about twelve months ago, by Low, and forced on board ; that he had got from one and another, whilst on board, about forty or fifty pounds, and that he had never been in the Bay since.

John Bright said he was a servant to one Hester, at the Bay, and there taken by Low and company, about three or four months since, and forced away to be their drummer.

Patrick Cunningham said, that about twelve months ago he was taken in a fishing schooner by Low and company, and forced away by them, and that at Newfoundland he endeavored to get away from them, was stopped, and retained by them ever since.

John Fletcher says, that he was a boy on board the Sycamore Galley, one Scott, commander, and he was taken out of her by Low and company, at Bonavista, because he could play upon the violin, and forced to be with them.

Thomas Child said, that in the beginning of March last

he was taken out of Captain Gilbert, at the Bay of Honduras, by Low and company, and was forced to go with them; they gave him a gun, (which he never used,) and fourteen or fifteen pounds, as near as he could remember, and one doubloon.

ADVOCATE GENERAL.

May it please your Honors,—I will not detain you with any particular reflections on the evidence, or upon the prisoners cases, differently circumstanced.

The court, I doubt not, will duly weigh and consider them, tempering justice with mercy, which sometimes is the true way to justice.

Then the prisoners were taken away from the bar, and all persons withdrawn from the court, save the Register.

The court having deliberately and maturely weighed and considered the evidences given against the prisoners, by a unanimous voice found the aforesaid Thomas Hazel, John Bright, and Patrick Cunningham, guilty of the piracies, robberies and felonies, exhibited against them, at this court. And John Fletcher, and Thomas Child, not guilty.

Then the prisoners being brought to the bar, the President told Thomas Hazel, John Bright, and Patrick Cunningham, that they were by a unanimous voice found guilty of piracies, robberies, and felonies, exhibited against them; and asked them if they had any thing to say, why sentence of death should not pass upon them, for their offences.

And the prisoners offering nothing material, the President pronounced sentence of death in the following words:

You Thomas Hazel, John Bright and Patrick Cunningham, are to go from hence to the place from whence you
came, from thence to the place of execution, and there
you, and each of you, are to be hanged by the neck, until
you are dead. And God in his infinite mercy, save your
souls.

The Articles of Agreement Between Low and his Company.

1st. The captain shall have two full shares, the master
a share and a half, the doctor, mate, gunner, carpenter,
and boatswain, a share and a quarter.

2d. He that shall be found guilty of striking or taking
up any unlawful weapon, either aboard of a prize or aboard
the privateer, shall suffer what punishment the Captain
and majority of the company shall think fit.

3d. He that shall be found guilty of cowardice, in time
of any engagement, shall suffer what punishment the
captain, and the majority of the company shall think fit.

5th. If any jewels, gold or silver, is found on board a
prize, to the value of a piece of eight, and the finder does
not deliver it to the quarter-master, in twenty-four hours
time, shall suffer what punishment the Captain and majority of the company shall see fit.

5th. He that shall be found guilty of gaming, or playing
at cards, or defrauding or cheating one another to the value
of a royal of plate, shall suffer what punishment the Captain, and a majority of the company shall think fit.

6th. He that shall be guilty of drunkenness, in the time
of an engagement, shall suffer what punishment the
Captain and majority of the company shall think fit.

7th. He that hath the misfortune to lose any of his limbs, in the time of an engagement, in the companies service, shall have the sum of six hundred pieces of eight, and kept in the company as long as he pleases.

8th. Good quarters to be given when craved.

9th. He that sees a sail first, shall have the best pistol, or small arm aboard of her.

10th. And lastly, no snapping of arms in the hold.

John Kencate, declared the above articles, to be the articles agreed upon, between Low and his company; to the best of his remembrance, having often seen them whilst with Low. Before, RICHARD WARD, Register.

The names, &c·, of the pirates that were executed, on Friday, July the 19th 1723, at Newport, on Rhode Island, at the place called Bull's Point, within the flux and reflux of the sea.

Names.	Age.	Place of Birth.
Charles Harris,		
Thomas Linnicar,	21	Lancaster, Eng.
Daniel Hyde,	23	Virginia.
Stephen Mundon,	29	London.
Abraham Lacy,	21	Devonshire, Eng.
Edward Lawson,	20	Isle of Man.
John Tompkins	21	Gloucester, Eng.
Francis Laughton;	39	New York.
John Fitzgerald,	27	O'Limb, Ireland.
William Studfield,	40	Lancaster, Eng.
Owen Rice,	27	South Wales.

25*

William Read,	25	Londonderry.
William Blades,	32	Rhode Island.
Thomas Hugget,	24	London.
Peter Cues,	32	Exon in Devon.
William Jones,	28	London.
Edward Eaton,	38	Weaxham.
John Brown,	27	Derham, Conn.
James Sprinkly,	28	Suffolk, Eng.
Joseph Sound,	28	Westminster City
Charles Church,	21	Mang, Par, Westin
John Waters,	35	County of Devon.
Thomas Powell,	21	Wethersfield.
Joseph Libbey,		
Thomas Hazel,		
John Bright.		

No. 4.—[p. 55.]
Bar Compact of 1745.

We the subscribers, considering that the law has made no distinction in fees between common, uncontroverted cases and those that are difficult in managing ; do for that end, and for regulating our practice in the law, and rendering the same sufficient for our support and subsistence, agree to the following rules, to be strictly kept up by us, upon honor.

I. No cause at any inferior court, where an answer is filed, shall be undertaken under forty shillings for a fee, or more.

II. No answer shall be filed under a forty shilling fee, besides payment of the charge of copies, &c.

III. No case to be pleaded at any Superior Court under a three pound fee.

IV. No writ of review to be brought under a four pound fee; and the same if for the defendant.

V. In the foregoing cases no man to be trusted without his note, saving a standing client, for whom considerable business is done.

VI. No Attorney to sign blank writs and disperse them about the colony, which practice, it is conceived, would make the law cheap, and hurt the business without profiting any one whatever.

VII. No Attorney shall take up any suit whatever against a practitioner who sues for his fees, except three or more brethren shall determine the demand unreasonable; and then if he will not do justice the whole fraternity shall rise up against him.

VIII. If any dispute should arise among the brethren about endorsement of writs for securing costs, it shall not be deemed a breach of unity, if one Attorney takes out a

torney shall become bail he is to expect no favor.

IX. No Attorney to advance money to pay entry and jury in cases disputed, except for a standing, responsible client, that happens to be out of the way.

At September Term, 1745.

DANIEL UPDIKE,
JAMES HONYMAN, Jr.,
JOHN APLIN,
JOHN WALTON,
MATTHEW ROBINSON,
DAVID RICHARDS, Jr.
THOMAS WARD,
JOHN ANDREWS.

Copied from the original manuscript, among the papers of the General Bar Meeting of Rhode-Island.

Per WILLIAM E. RICHMOND,

Secretary of Providence County Bar.

No. 5.—[152.] ⁓

[Extract from the Journals of the old Congress.]

"Tuesday, November 4, 1777."

"*Resolved,* That Congress have a high sense of the merit of Colonel Greene, and the officers and men under his command, in their late defence of Fort Mercer, on the river Delaware, and that an elegant sword be provided by the Board of War, and presented to Colonel Greene.

"*Resolved,* That Congress have a high sense of the merits of Lieutenant Colonel Smith, and the officers and men under his command, in their late gallant defence of Fort Mifflin, on the river Delaware, and that an elegant sword be provided by the Board of War, and presented to Lieutentant Colonel Smith.

"*Resolved,* That Congress have a high sense of the merits of Commodore Hazlewood, commander of the naval force on the Delaware river, in the service of the Commonwealth of Pennsylvania, and of the officers and men under his command, in their late gallant defence of their country against the British fleet, whereby two of their men of war were destroyed, and four others were compelled to retire ; and that an elegant sword be provided by the Marine Committee, and presented to Commodore Hazlewood.".

No. 6.—[154.]

Letter from General Varnum on the conduct of Major Thayer.

Mr. Wheeler.—The rewards of merit are ever grateful to generous minds; and when bestowed by the representative sovereignty of a nation, create the most exalted attachments. Happy, therefore, must every virtuous citizen have been, in observing the names of those worthy officers, mentioned in your paper of the 15th of June last, whom Congress have honored with distinguished marks of their approbation! From public testimonials of this kind, [however exalted may be our veneration for the character of the individuals, and too exalted it cannot be,] we should not forget that others, equally deserving, although perhaps not equally conspicuous. My design, by this address, is to rescue from seeming inattention, the brilliant conduct of Colonel, the late Major Thayer, in the defence of Mud Island, in the river Delaware, from the 12th of November until the 16th of the same month, in the year 1777. To a person unacquainted with that transaction, all the glory would be ascribed to Col. Smith, of the Maryland line. He is a gentleman of superior talents, of fine sentiments, virtuous, and brave! He commanded the garrison, upon Mud Island, from the latter part of September, excepting a few days, till the 11th of November, when the command devolved upon Lieut, Col. Russell, of the Connecticut line. The fatigues and dan-

gers of that command were extreme. Colonel Smith supported them with uncommon patience and fortitude, but
yielded to hard necessity. Lieutenant Colonel Russell,
an amiable, sensible man, and an excellent officer, exhausted by fatigue, and totally destitute of health, requested to be recalled. The moment was critical. The commander-in-chief, his Excellency General Washington, had
not an idea of holding the place through the campaign ;
but wished to retard the operations of the enemy until the
main army should be reinforced by the Massachusetts
brigade marching from the conquest of Saratoga, when he
would be in sufficient force to cover the country, or meet
the enemy's whole force in the field. Upon the 12th,
therefore, he signified his orders to the commanding General, at Woodberry, on the Jersey side, who had the direction of all the forces below Philadelphia, to defend the
island as long as possible without sacrificing the garrison.
To defend it was absolutely impossible, unless the siege
could be raised by an attack upon the besiegers from the
main army. This was deemed impracticable by a general
council of war, and therefore not farther considered as an
ultimate object. Nothing could then present itself to a
relieving officer, fully informed of all the circumstances,
but certain death, or an improbable escape, without the
possibility of contending upon equal terms. The love of
our country may lead us to the field of battle, ambition
may lead us to particular enterprises ; but magnanimity
alone can soar above every danger! The commanding
General could not detach an officer in rotation ; his reasons
were insuperable. In a moment so critical, when every
thing dear to his feelings required an immediate decision,
happy for him, and more happy for the United States,

Major Thayer presented himself as a volunteer! The of-

the 12th to the morning of the 16th of November, he defended the island with the greatest address, against a fu-
rious and almost continued cannonade and bombardment
from a variety of batteries at small distances. The defences at best were trifling, the place itself was illy chosen ; Hog Island and Billingsport instead of Mud Island

whole British force was displayed from their land batter-

sustained and repelled the shock with astonishing intre-
pidity, for several hours, assisted from our gallies and batteries on the Jersey shore. By the middle of the day,
these defences were leveled with the common mud, and
the gallant officers and men philosophically expected each
others fate in the midst of carnage.

The Grenadiers and Light Infantry of the British were
paraded on the opposite shore, and the Vigilant, an India-
man cut down to a battery of 20 twenty-four pounders
on one side, lay within twenty yards of the troops.
The attack was incessant ; two attempts, from our gallies,
were unsuccessfully made to board the Vigilant. The
commanding General was determined to fight the enemy
on the island, if the Vigilant could be taken ; she could
not, then nothing remained but securing the garrison,
whose distance from the enemy on both sides was not half
so far as from the body of his troops upon the shore.
During this day more than one thousand and thirty dis-
charges of cannon, from thirty-two to twelve pounders,
were made in twenty minutes. Such a day America
never saw till then !

Early in the evening of the 15th, Major Thayer dispatched all his garrison, less than three hundred in number, to the shore, excepting forty, with whom he remained, braving death itself. At twelve at night, between the 15th and 16th, the barracks were fired, all the military stores being previously sent away, and the Major and his brave companions, he being the last from the scene of slaughter, arrived at Red Bank, to the joy and astonishment of all the army.

The subscriber was personally knowing to all the facts before related, and therefore begs of you to publish them. He may have varied in some minute instances, but materially he hath not. Should any of these facts be disputed, he will publish an attested narrative which will silence envy itself.

Should other printers, who have published the first mentioned honorary testimonials, see this, they will oblige the writer in publishing it also.

JAMES M. VARNUM.

East Greenwich, August 2, 1786."

————

No. 7.—[216.]

Letter from James M. Varnum, of Rhode-Island, to the President of the Federal Convention, enclosing a communication from certain citizens of Rhode-Island.

NEWPORT, June 18th, 1787.

Sir,—The enclosed address, of which I presume your Excellency has received a duplicate, was returned to me from New-York, after my arrival in this state. I flattered myself that our legislature, which convened on Monday last, would have receded from the resolution referred to and have complied with the resolution of Congress in sending delegates to the Federal Convention. The upper House, or Governor and Council, embraced the measure, but it was negatived in the Assembly by a large majority, notwithstanding that the greatest exertions were made to support it.

Being disappointed in their expectations, the minority in the administration, and all the worthy citizens of the state, whose minds are well informed, regretting the peculiarity of their situation, place the fullest confidence in the wisdom and moderation of the National council, and indulge the warmest hopes of being favorably considered in their deliberation. From these deliberations they anticipate a political system which must finally be adopted, and from which will result the safety, the honor, and the happiness of the United States.

Permit me, Sir, to observe that the measures of our legislature do not exhibit the real character of the state. They are equally reprobated and abhorred by gentlemen of the learned professions, by the whole mercantile body, and by the most respectable farmers and mechanics. The majority of the administration are composed of a licentious body of men, destitute of education, and many of them void of principle. From anarchy and confusion they derive a temporary consequence, and this they endeavor to prolong by debauching the minds of the common people, whose attention is wholly directed to the abolition of debts, public and private. With these are associated the disaffected of all parties, particularly those

26

who were unfriendly during the war. Their paper money system, founded in oppression and fraud, they are determined to support at every hazard; and rather than relinquish their favorite project, they trample upon the most sacred obligations. As a proof of this, they refused to comply with the requisition of Congress for repealing all laws repugnant to the treaty of peace with Great Britain; and urged as their principal reason that it would be calling in question the propriety of their former measures.

These may be attributed partly to the extreme freedom of our Constitution, and partly to the want of energy in the Federal union; and it is greatly to be apprehended that they cannot be speedily removed, but by uncommon and very serious exertions. It is fortunate, however, that the wealth and resources of the state are chiefly in possession of the well affected, and that they are entirely devoted to the public good.

I have the honor to be, Sir, with the greatest veneration and esteem, your Excellency's very obedient and faithful servant,

J. M. VARNUM.

His Excellency GEN. WASHINGTON.

No. VIII.—[p. 232.]

WESTERLY, R. I., Oct. 25th, 1841.

Dear Sir,—I am in receipt of your letter of recent date, in which you request the particulars of a conversation with the celebrated Thomas Paine, in relation to Gen. Varnum, formerly a distinguished citizen of our state.

ington, as well as some account of Nathan Haley — to which it seems, from your remarks, I have, in our social intercourse, at some time alluded. As far as recollection may serve, I will briefly detail these particulars. They are but few, and to minds less eager of anecdote than yours, they must be of minor importance. In the summer of 1803, Thomas Paine was a sojourner in Stonington, Connecticut, on a visit to his friend Haley, a native

and that intimacy conferred on Stonington the benefits of that visit. Haley had his birth on the east bank of Mystic river ; his parents were too confiding in nature to think of involving the agency of art, or authority, to restrain the bold and eccentric sallies of a spirited youth. His early days were marked with deeds of daring, and in riper years, as a mariner, he rose to the rank of a ship's commander. He was but little indebted to early education, while native talents gave him currency among the better informed, and evinced his capacity for business. His mental and physical energies were of no ordinary character. The French revolution naturally attracted him to its scenes, for he loved the confusion of war. He served with distinction as an officer in the navy of France, and was one of Buonparte's Legion of Honor. It must be admitted, however, that some of his deeds, consistent as they may have been with his code of honor, were of doubtful morality—yet his whole life was interspersed with occasional acts of benevolence and kindness. His native country confided to him the American Consulate at Nantes, in France, where he lived and died within the present year. Thomas Paine's arrival at Stonington, afforded meet occasion for the Democracy of that town to light up its altar. His political writings, which stimulated the American revolution, were in vivid recollection. The Federal administration had gone over to Democracy, while the fond hope of putting down the old Federalists of Connecticut, with whom they were then struggling in the spirit of revolution, awakened every kindred sympathy, and the advent of Paine seemed a favorable presage of that success. Dinner parties were made for him, and here I should be ungrateful did I not aver, that Stonington vies with the whole world for generous and noble hospitality. My local proximity was favorable to my connection with these festive boards. I had the honor to be introduced as a lawyer from Rhode-Island, which, as you naturally would suppose, gave me a ready passport to the respectful notice of the distinguished guest. His enquiries after Rhode-Island and her leading men, with whom he had once entertained intercourse, bespoke his kind regard for the state. On one occasion while at dinner, his enquiries were very particular after Gen. Varnum. I informed him that the General died at Marietta, on the Ohio. He said he had on many occasions listened to him as a public speaker with great delight. He characterized the style of his oratory even to the musical intonations of his voice. He said he had listened to many of the best speakers in America and Europe, and that in point of charming elocution, James Mitchell Varnum was the most eloquent man he ever heard speak, and he thought it strange that his name had not attained more celebrity. In relation to Mr. Paine, I have never expected that I should become his biographer, and of course have not gathered materials for that work. I can state to you only what fell under my own observation. He was a man about sixty-six years old, of middling stature, easy of access and free in conversation. His topics were national and political, on all of which he was sensible, though not eloquent. Sometimes he aimed at wit, and now and then *slopt* over a low jest or sarcasm on the bible and on the priesthood. But those irreverent jeers elicited no responses of congenial sentiment among those about him. They recognized him only in his political character. His speculations on theology were abstractions too remote and contingent for the practical worldly notions and business habits of Stonington. An elegant *fish dinner*, accompanied with exhilerating *et ceteras*, at that day, was void of offence, and with reverberating acclamations of Jefferson and liberty, seemed glory enough for those who entertained Tom Paine.

With great respect your friend,
NATHAN F. DIXON.

W. Updike, Esq.

No. IX.—[p. 247.]

Cambridge, 23d May, 1837.

Dear Sir,—In my reply to your letter of the 20th instant, I have to regret that I am unable to gratify your request relative to the personal and professional characters of our distinguished lawyers. I can, however, mention the names of several judges and pleaders of eminence whom you have omitted to name—namely, Augustus Johnson, who was Attorney General and Stamp master.

I saw his effigy, and that of another lawyer, Martin Howard, and Dr. Moffat, hanged, and afterwards burnt on the
Newport parade, and the contents of their houses and
cellars destroyed by a mob at night.

Of gentlemen of the law, I would mention Judge
Scott, Judge Hazard, William Ellery, Mr. Simpson, an
Englishman, who was saved from a ship laden with
rum that took fire and burnt on entering the harbor, with
a number of comedians of both sexes. Simpson practised law in Rhode-Island, and died in England among other
refugees; Walter Channing, father of William Ellery
Channing, D. D., of Boston, Judge Howell, Judge Helme,
of Narragansett. Henry Bull I can just remember when
I was a small boy. I knew Judge Lightfoot very well.
He was * * * * a Judge of Admiralty—a very well educated, idle man. I knew his sisters in London, single and
opulent. He first taught me to value and study Lord
Bacon, and from him I learnt to value Locke, Newton and
Boerhaave. He was the oracle of literary men in Newport. After more than seven years absence in Europe, he
called upon me in this town of Cambridge. He was a
very able and learned man, and at Rhode-Island, I thought

Condemned to trudge,
Without an equal, and without a judge.

He was a great epicure, a perfect living encycloypædia,
and welcome at the table of the first characters—and constantly dined from home. He was not a buffoon, or mimic;
but a fine relater of apt anecdotes. He informed every
body and contradicted no one, but had a happy Socratic
method of teaching. He honored me by his notice; and
I gathered more knowledge from him, than from any other
man in the choice of books. I am not certain that he

ever read law as a pofession, yet he was master of it, as
well as of the science of medicine; and in the highest
parpxysm of party politics, he had the rare art of veiling
his contempt. Next to Dr. Fothergill, I owe Judge Lightfoot more than any other man I can name. He taught me
to strip off the husk and break the shell of the *cocoa-nut*
of learning, so as to come at the meat. During thirty
years that I gave lectures in this University of Cambridge,
I endeavored to display the pages of LOCKE, BACON, and
LINNÆUS, but should hardly been able to have done what
little I have, had I never known Lightfoot.

Of Henry Bull, I have heard many a pleasant anecdote
from my father, and so also of William Ellery, both face-
tious characters. I have scattered hints of this sort to my
worthy friend, the Rev. Mr. Elton, which he may use as
he thinks fit. I suspect by your name, or rather *Opdyke,*
that your ancestors were Dutch—the wisest people in
Europe, in my opinion.

It does not follow that every Judge amongst us is a
learned man. My father, e. g., was a Judge in the Court
of Common Pleas, but was not a lawyer by profession,
nor even a man of public education. It was with Judges
fifty years ago, as with physicians, before we taught by
lectures.

I have seen Dr. McSparran; there is a good picture of
him in his canonicals. He was a jocose, loud talking man.
Some of the FAIRWEATHERS are still living in this town,
and some of your GORTONS. I write this on the spur of
the occasion and rapidly, and errors of the pen may be
the consequence.

Honyman was a gentlemen of the old school. He

had an enormous wen like a Swiss, hanging from his under jaw, too large for extirpation. Marchant was likewise a gentleman of the old school, and Bradford and Varnum, a popular aspirant. Also John Cooke, Marchant's brother-in-law. Ellery and his three brothers, were flaming sons of liberty, in the Stamp act period, while Martin Howard was on the opposite side. Howard died Chief Justice of South Carolina. A fine portrait of him is in the Boston Court House.

I give you all my recollections, and write this in haste, so as to send my letter by the morning's mail, and remain with friendly and respectful salutations, yours,

BENJAMIN WATERHOUSE.

No X.

CAMBRIDGE, Nov. 24th 1839.

Sir,—In reply to your letter of the 19th inst. I remark, in the language of tailors, that you have cut out more work for me than I could make up in a fortnight. Judge Lightfoot I knew intimately and long; he was a man of sense, an Oxford scholar, in the prime of life as to understanding and perfectly at leisure, having, as I learnt in London, never been brought up to any occupation. He was, for many years, a leading man in a sort of club, or coterie, at Newport, under the unpopular name of "Tories." Honyman was, in my day, an old and respectable lawyer. Augustus Johnson, a man of wit and popular talents—take one trait of it. He was prosecuting for an assault and battery, when in justifying the person, who gave the first blow, he said, that if the Apostle Paul himself were upon earth, and was to strike him, he would have *one lick at the old fellow, if he were damned for it the next moment.* William B. Simpson was an Englishman, and belonged originally to a troop of comedians, who came from one of the West India-Islands. I met him and his wife in London, amongst the unhappy refugees, subsisting on a small pittance from the government.

Would it not be worth your while to save from oblivion some of the respectable family of Wantons, several of whom were Governors from the earliest settlement of the colony down to the burning of the British ship Gaspee? We ought, in gratitude, to honor the name and family of Abraham Redwood, founder of its once very fine library, which is still very valuable, and which I wish my friend Christopher Champlin would, for he can, keep from oblivion and shame.

I am glad to find that there is a disposition to keep up the character and consequence of the Redwood Library. It was long the most valuable collection in the American colonies, and ought not only to be kept up, but increased by a steady stream of benevolence. I am persuaded that my old and valued friend Christopher G. Champlin will never suffer that intellectual stream to dry up, or even to run low. His having no offspring is a strong natural argument, joined to others, that he should keep the literary character of a *natale solum.* He has not arrived, by a considerable space, to that period, when the *grasshopper* is a burthen. The Redwood Library is even yet an elegant monument of judicious bounty and liberality.

Is there no literary man, clergyman or layman, at Rhode-

Island, who would stretch forth his liberal hand to preserve
the renown of Bishop Berkeley from fading? I am pretty
confident that the name of Redwood will not fade, nor
that of some of the benevolent Jews. Newport will be
—must be, in time, the *Bath* of the United States, to
which rich invalids will retire for lost health. I often wished that I had some pleasant spot, or farm, on my native island, to which, if not myself, my invalid posterity might resort to enjoy peace, health and liberty. That Newport, or
rather the whole island, will ultimately form the grand
naval depot of our nation, is so probable, that it approxi-
mates almost to a certainty. Dr. Fothergill, my valued
friend, and almost father, had that idea. His sudden and
unexpected death cut short some of his steps towards it.
I often figure to myself what the grand estuary of Rhode-
Island will be, when it will connect Fall River and
Taunton, and Milton and Braintree bay, or rather the Massachusetts Bay, shall form the grand depot of the north,
backed and supported by a matchless militia extending
from Narragansett bay to Penobscot.

As the small pox is frightening the people of Boston
and its vicinity, many are incessantly calling upon me to
show their old scars of vaccination, from a notion that I
can tell by its appearance, and especially whether they be
safe from a future infection; for if any one has got his
name up for any thing, the people are too apt to believe
whatever he may say on the subject of enquiry. It is
now nearly sixty years since I vaccinated the first patients
—my own children—from the very room and table where
I am now sitting, and have thereby nearly exterminated
one of the most odious and dreadfnl plagues that ever af-

fected mankind. I once innoculated all the inhabitants of Newport, who would accept of that blessing. The places of worship, particularly your Trinity church, were the places where they convened for that purpose. I mention this to you as a Recorder or Historian of Rhode-Island, for such things should not escape even a public record. The carelessness of people on such subjects is lamentable. The Rev. Mr. Dehone preached two sermons on that subject, in my hearing, at Newport; and it is now time that the same subject should be revived, and the salutiferous practice revived, for the longer it is neglected, the less chance will there be of forever keeping the Rhode-Island people free from one of the most loathsome of plagues.

I hint these things from a strong desire to preserve the inhabitants of my native place from one of the most terrible scourges that ever afflicted mankind, the plague itself not excepted.

I have written the foregoing with a rapid pen, and for the best of purposes; for being now nearer *ninety* than *eighty*, I am anxious that my native place should have all the benefits that may result from the experience of their affectionate son.   BENJAMIN WATERHOUSE.

P. S. I keep but a short memorandum of this letter, and leave you to notice it in your own way. It needs a criticising eye, especially as the latter part of it is written by candle light. The source of your information may be mentioned in your way.   B. W.

W. Updike, Esq.

CPSIA information can be obtained at www.ICGtesting.com
Printed in the USA
BVOW02s0816010915

416039BV00011B/117/P

9 781331 434153